Uphill

Uphill

A Personal Story

Eleanor McGovern

with
Mary Finch Hoyt

Illustrated with Photographs

Houghton Mifflin Company Boston 1974

A portion of this book has
appeared in *Good Housekeeping.*

FIRST PRINTING   V

Library of Congress Cataloging in Publication Data
McGovern, Eleanor, 1921–
    Uphill; a personal story.
    1. McGovern, Eleanor, 1921–   2. McGovern,
George Stanley, 1922–   I. Hoyt, Mary Finch,
joint author.   II. Title.
E840.8.M338A38   328.73'092'4 [B]   74-11065
ISBN   0-395-19414-8

Printed in the United States of America

TO OUR FAMILIES,

WHO HAVE HELPED US TO GROW.

E. McG. & M.F.H.

Contents

Illustrations

The family farm on the plains outside Woonsocket, South Dakota, where Eleanor McGovern grew up.

Eleanor's parents, Marion Payne Stegeberg and Earl Stegeberg.

Eleanor and her twin sister, Ila, in 1922.

Eleanor and Ila at the age of seven, with their mother and little sister, Phyllis.

Eleanor and Ila at their high school graduation in Woonsocket, 1939.

Pinning on Lieutenant George McGovern's wings at Flight Cadet School graduation in Pampa, Texas, 1943.

George and Eleanor McGovern, reunited after the war years.

The McGovern family in Mitchell, South Dakota, in the mid-1950's. *AP Wirephoto*

The McGovern family during George's first Congressional campaign in 1956.

Freshman Congressman and Mrs. George S. McGovern, photographed before attending President Eisenhower's second Inaugural Ball, January 20, 1957.

At the Democratic National Convention in Chicago, August, 1968:

The wives of the three major candidates — Abigail Mc-Carthy, Muriel Humphrey, Eleanor McGovern. *United Press International*

Eleanor McGovern with her family before her first press conference at the Blackstone Hotel ballroom. *Chicago Tribune*

Eleanor and her son Steve, watching the end of the 1968 Convention on TV in the McGovern suite at the Blackstone Hotel. *Time-Life, Inc.*

The McGoverns at home in Washington before the 1972 Democratic National Convention. *Stanley Tretick*

At Miami Beach during the 1972 Convention:

Eleanor and Ila. *Stanley Tretick*

In the McGoverns' Doral Hotel Suite, George and his grandson Matthew. *Stanley Tretick*

Eleanor and Teresa. *Stanley Tretick*

Eleanor happily waving to the crowds from the family box in Convention Hall just after George had won the nomination on the night of July 12. *Wide World Photos*

Working and learning during the Presidential campaign:

On a "listening tour" in a Baltimore dress factory, Eleanor takes shorthand notes in one of her black notebooks. *Stuart Bratesman*

Eleanor visits the Children's Center in Oakland, California.

Uphill

Chapter I

Homecoming

SHORTLY AFTER DUSK on October 17, 1972, a gentle snow began to fall over my little hometown of Woonsocket, South Dakota.

Soon the National Guard Armory would come alive as the Woonsocket High School band and the singing Highlanders from Dakota Wesleyan University set up their folding chairs down in front of the stage and the auditorium filled up with South Dakotans, Iowans, and Minnesotans, some from as far away as a hundred miles, for "Welcome Home, Eleanor" night.

I felt a certain ambivalence about the homecoming planned for me. There was the anticipation of being with dear ones, but I was embarrassed by all the fuss. Besides, the Presidential election was only three weeks off. It was not a good time to stop, even momentarily,

----

the relentless pace believed to be essential for our national campaign.

That afternoon my staff, a Secret Service detail, some reporters, and I — the usual contingent for a candidate's wife — had flown from Washington to Chicago to Sioux Falls, South Dakota. The local press was waiting at the airport.

Question: What will happen to the Democrats if President Nixon ends the war before November seventh?

Answer: I hope he does. Some things are just above and beyond the campaign, and that's one.

Question: What if your husband loses?

Answer: He likes being the Senator from South Dakota; however, we haven't discussed defeat. He expects to win.

Question: If he does win, what about your plans to be the White House child advocate?

Answer: That is too involved to go into here.

The airport press conference, followed by an hour-and-a-half drive to Mitchell and a swing past the Corn Palace — the town's unexpectedly fanciful auditorium and visitors' center whose walls are huge Midwest murals intricately worked in dried corn and grain — had wiped out dinner on the schedule. In fact, there had barely been time to register at the Holiday Inn in Mitchell, change clothes, and form another mini-motorcade for the thirty-four-mile drive home.

Once on the road toward Woonsocket for the last leg of the trip, I settled back into the corner of the limousine. If I looked out the window, I could avoid conversation with Mary Hoyt and Margot Hahn, my press secretary and my next-door neighbor, who were always with me; Skip Williams and Denise Ferrenz, Secret Service agents on duty in the front seat, never intruded, even with encouragement. I would have time to gather my thoughts at last.

We sped quietly down the road in the dusky fall evening. On either side the cornfields slipped past, edged by shelter belts planted after the dust-bowl droughts to keep the black soil from drifting, the first of each protective row planted in lilacs. Behind a farmhouse I thought I recalled loomed a gleaming silo; at the fork of a road was the County Correction Line I remembered well.

People are often curious about South Dakota, and I like to boast that my state has "the longest unnavigable river in the world," "the deepest artesian well," "the hundredth busiest airport." When George started speaking out about the war, deploring the immensity of the military budget, he pointed out that "if South Dakota were to secede from the Union and become an independent country, with its one hundred and sixty Minuteman missiles, its Strategic Air Command base, it would become the third-ranking nuclear power in the world." Superlatives about our state still come easily to both of us, even after a million miles of travel in other regions of the country.

Out on the road east of town we pulled over to see a sign. It was painted lavender, the color possibly chosen because in South Dakota lilacs grow in profusion or perhaps because the little state flower, the pasqueflower, is purple. The edges of the sign were bordered with lacy white around the part that read "Woonsocket: Hometown of Eleanor McGovern." I had not seen it before. My dad would have been pleased, but he would have appreciated even more the announcement later that evening that "actually, Eleanor is a Cuthbert girl. The farm was six miles from Cuthbert and eight miles from Woonsocket. The only difference is that Woonsocket is still here. Cuthbert is part of Martin Neilsen's farm."

Eight miles out of town was a considerable distance in those days, and my twin sister, Ila, and I moved into Woonsocket during weekdays and took turns going out to the farm on weekends. We could afford to go to high school if we lived with the Darrell Parsons, who gave us room and board in exchange for housework. Now our motorcade drove past the Parsons' brown shingle house on Highway 34, its broad front porch closer to the street than I had remembered. Mr. Parsons was dead and Mrs. Parsons had moved to Huron. If they had been there, I would have stopped. I chronically hate to get up in the morning, and it has something to do with days in that house when one of my jobs had been to get up early each day to iron a clean shirt for Mr. Parsons to wear to his creamery.

In my teen years there was not time to worry about

life balancing out. There were special times and there were normal times. But today I am more aware of the juxtapositions of love and deprivation in my childhood, of freedom and responsibility in my youth, and of tenderness and chaos in my maturing years. Without these myriad strands it would have been more difficult, I know, to accept the different drives and natures of five children, to support a gentle, questing man as he moved from teaching to the ministry to politics, and to keep something in reserve for myself.

Places change, but my closest friends and relatives seem always to stay the same. About twenty-five of them were waiting for me in the steamy kitchen of my younger sister, Phyllis, who lives around the corner from the Woonsocket Armory: Uncle Alger Payne and Aunt Myrtle, Eddie Swenson, Alice Parsons Jones, Bev and Tom Morris, former students of George's, and friends from nearby Huron, Mitchell, and Fulda, Minnesota. We hugged one another and they gave me a big white orchid nestled in pink roses.

They had planned an unscheduled stop on the way to the Armory, even if it meant being a few minutes late for the giant party. Like most small communities today, whose ill and aging citizens need special care outside of their homes, Woonsocket has built a modern nursing facility. It is a block from Phyllis' house. For years in political campaigns I have toured similar centers and talked with old people about their concerns. But that night was truly special. In the center, ablaze with lights, crowded with ambulatory and wheel-

chair patients who had gathered to wait for me, some
playing checkers, others sitting quietly around the
pleasant public rooms, were men and women with
worn, familiar faces, whose opinions and reputations I
had valued in my years of growing up.

I knew many of them, and Mrs. Tom Callan, the
head nurse, introduced me to the others. Edward Jo-
hansen was the first person I recognized. He was a
farmer friend of Dad's. Alex Parquet was there. Avis
Gibbs had brought her green parrot, who wouldn't
keep still, and Clara Webster and another friend had
stitched up two sweet, droopy dolls from circlets of
gingham for me to take home to the grandchildren.

We had separate little chats. "Do you remember
me?" they asked. "I knew your folks real well," one
woman said. "Good luck to you and your husband."
Then it was time to go.

Woonsocket's population is only about eight
hundred and I was touched to find that at least fifteen
hundred people had showed up for the occasion,
which was supposed to be bipartisan, even though the
master of ceremonies, Les Helgeland, announced immediately that he was a registered Republican newspaper editor whose paper disagreed with George's politics, and I had to remind him publicly that he was my
cousin!

Onstage I looked out over the rows of old school-
mates, girlhood chums, long-time friends, and close
and distant relatives, some smiling and waving,
others nodding happily when our eyes caught.

*"Well, hello, Eleanor, hello, Eleanor, you're still goin',
you're still glowin', you're still goin' strong,"* the Woonsocket choral group sang briskly. I was self-conscious
because I knew I wasn't glowing at all. In fact, I was
unnaturally pale, my weight had fallen off to ninety-
three pounds, and it had been publicized nationally that
I had been recently hospitalized after near collapse as
speaker at a Jefferson-Jackson Day dinner in Frederick, Maryland, where I followed a minister who called
upon the Lord to "help us to roll up our sleeves and
get in there and slug it out for the things we believe."
I had been slugging it out for twenty-four months,
campaigning alone, for the most part. Most recently I
had not seen George for two weeks, as I had been traveling on a separate schedule on the West Coast for
eight days — 7169 miles, according to reporters with
me — sometimes hitting three cities a day for sixteen
or eighteen hours without rest. Out in California a
McGovern supporter standing near me in the hot sun
at a press conference, a giant of a man with a small
child perched on his shoulders, had sensed my growing fatigue. "Mrs. McGovern, if you're wearing out,"
he said earnestly, "I'll *personally* carry you through this
campaign." McGovern supporters were like that.

"You're still goin' strong," the chorus echoed, and
then Larry Ball, the student body president, gave me
six red roses and introduced Mayor Ira Merriman,
who presented me first with the key to the city and
then to our dear friend, Lieutenant Governor Bill
Dougherty, who brought tears to my eyes when he

spoke about the "honor" George and I brought to the state. By the time the vocal group sang "Let there be peace, and let it begin with me," followed by "This land is your land, this land is my land," George's campaign song, there must have been color in my cheeks.

Before every speech I am like a neophyte actress on opening night. I can't eat, I feel sick, and I am sure I cannot go through with it. But once I am on my feet, nervousness disappears and I enjoy elaborating and digressing in an extemporaneous style that sometimes prolongs my speeches for twice as long as planned. I always seem to be "winging it," either from necessity or by choice. I need to relate to an audience, and I am not comfortable until I emphasize that I have strong views, reflecting the evolving nature of my life, but am not a professional anything. Very often the formless thoughts that please me most, the insights that fit the moment best, struggle into shape right on stage.

Mary Kay, my seventeen-year-old daughter, had written a poem for the occasion. It was called "Going Home," and I began by reading it.

> I am a traveler who will always roam
> To cities and places not my own
> The hours are weary when I am alone
> But now I return to my heart, to my home.
>
> The prairies and farmland where tall grasses grew
> The people I loved and the times we knew
> My family and friends that taught me the truth
> My home, I am coming, I am coming to you.
>
> The places I saw as a child so young
> The shining soft colors of a setting sun

The blue open sky, like no other one
My home.
"Those are magic words," I said. And with the
thoughts of my home one memory led to another: my
first day at Slack School in Twin Lakes with Cousin Les
and his sisters; Alfred Godfrey, my first teacher; my
funny first high school double date with Ila; the debating team; cheering the Redmen on; and the night
George McGovern first met Earl Stegeberg, my father.
My thoughts of George were strong. Even at the risk
of injecting what could be construed as politics, I had
to say a few personal words about him.

"Many wonderful things happen on the campaign," I
told the Woonsocket audience. "As I go through a
crowd people thrust things into my hands — five-
dollar bills, twenty-dollar bills, a cross. But the most
beautiful experience is to go through a crowd and hear
people say, 'We love your husband,' or 'We need your
husband.' And this is what I have been hearing. I
wonder how many Presidential candidates in history
have heard those words — 'We love you'?"

Months after the election, in spite of criticism and
rejection we could hardly endure, many, many people — many who did not even vote for George — went
out of their way to show us signs of friendship: at airports, at the movies, in the supermarket, even at a
highway traffic light in Virginia where a truck driver
suddenly called out to me, "Thank you, and thank the
Senator." In Oneonta, New York, after a commence-
ment speech in 1973, I went back to my motel and
found a warm rhubarb pie a woman had baked for me

to take home to George and a bottle of Vitamin C for me from a man who had heard me sneeze. One weekend, after we had crossed the ferry to our country cottage on Maryland's Eastern Shore, we discovered the words "I love you, Senator" printed on the inexcusably dusty door of George's car by a stranger who signed her name in the grime, "Ann Gillelan."

My black notebooks are full of the names of strangers who have been kind to us. I carry these loose-leaf binders wherever I go so that I can scribble down in shorthand names, places, quotations, poems, or experiences that mean something to me. I had leafed through page after page on the night before we flew to Woonsocket, searching for my theme. It was an evening for sharing thoughts, not for rhetoric about the war, taxes, the economy, or for serious analysis of what was then dismissed as the "Watergate Caper."

"Those of us with a home to come home to are the lucky ones," I began, recalling the words of a friend who had told me when she learned I was coming back to Woonsocket that it must be "wonderful to know where your roots are" because "I don't know where mine are."

"I learned to accept responsibility at an early age. Everyone did in my time. And so I have never feared taking responsibility. I felt useful, and I never doubted it. Let's not underestimate the importance of feeling needed.

"As I travel the length and breadth of this land, over and over again people say to me, 'I don't feel wanted' or 'Where is my place?' The most important thing I learned as a child here in Woonsocket was that there was always a place for me — in my family, in my community, in my country.

"Family, community, country — these should be welcome places. To be useful is what matters." I was reminded of these thoughts a few months after the 1972 election, when I was picking up the threads of my life again but had lost all zest or confidence. I had delivered a speech to a Head Start group in Chicago and had been introduced by Dr. Naomi Abrams of the University of Chicago, who left early but sent this cheering message: "Tell Eleanor it is good to have her back in the struggle." How reassuring it was to feel welcome! For my Woonsocket upbringing says that we are too valuable to sit by the side of the road and watch the parade go by.

That is what I was trying to say to my hometown friends before they went out into the snowy night.

Chapter II

A Buried City

O<small>N THE WAY BACK</small> to Sioux Falls the next morning, as our motorcade streaked down a highway treacherously encrusted with ice patches glinting in the brilliant sun, I was so depressed that I actually wept.

All around was evidence of change. Only an abandoned farm here and there was reminiscent of my girlhood on the drought-stricken plains, when my father struggled grimly to save our farm as neighbors all around us lost theirs.

Actually, we had a thriving farm, as thriving as a 320-acre farm could be in depression days. And my mother and father, my sisters Ila and Phyllis, and I, lived in a big, eight-room frame house with porches upstairs and down, and lilacs in the yard. I was proud of our house. We did not have running water, electric-ity, or central heating, but we had a furnace that burned corncobs if we could not afford coal or wood, and Mother had a washing machine with a motor, kept in perfect running order by Dad, instead of a contraption that needed to be cranked by hand like other folks we knew.

It never occurred to me that we were poor or that I was deprived, even after tragedy transformed my life when I was eleven years old. How different was my childhood, when traveling thirty miles was high adventure and an ice-cream cone a luxury, from the early years of my own children and grandchildren! Back in Washington that morning after my homecoming in Woonsocket, my oldest daughter, Ann Mead, twenty-seven, who had slept in a dresser drawer in a tiny, two-room apartment when she was a baby, was probably feeding my youngest grandson, Kevin, four months, in our modern kitchen with its center aisle for built-in electric stove, dishwasher, clothes washer and dryer, while blond and beautiful Timmy, two years, might be watering the chrysanthemums from a plastic can on the sun deck of our hillside Japanese house in Northwest Washington, described to our embarrassment in news reports as having custom-made furniture, sliding shoji, fusuma rice-paper walls, and an enormous price tag.

Sue, twenty-six, and her husband, Jim Rowen, would be packing for the campaign trail with blue-eyed Matthew, six months, who had been nursed and diapered by his liberated mother at political rallies, coffees, and press conferences across the country, and

even on the "Dakota Queen II," George's campaign
plane, and in Constitution Hall at a fund-raising gala.

Teresa, twenty-three, who had moved to Charlottesville, Virginia, in 1968 to study and work and get professional help for some personal problems that had
culminated in her arrest for possession of marijuana,
would be back in Washington for a few days preparing
to take off for a six-day, six-state campaign tour of the
Deep South in Liz Carpenter's converted camper,
"Grassroots Grasshopper." Mary Kay, seventeen, who
had recently converted to Catholicism in spite of her
Methodist Sunday School days, I hoped would be in
class, making up credits so that she could graduate
from Bethesda-Chevy Chase High School. And Steve,
twenty, our talented only son, looking desperately for a
path to his future, undoubtedly was fiddling with his
electric guitar while he weighed the decision to get a
job or go to college.

My family — we were being analyzed, criticized,
scrutinized, and described as "a microcosm of the real-
life situations that countless other American families
face today," as "seventies people" whose "lives have
reflected the uncertainties and frustrations known to
millions of Americans in recent years." And I worried
about the unforeseeable pressure on all of us to share
with the public those personal "uncertainties and frustrations." I knew that millions of Americans might be
able to relate to us, to empathize because we, as a public family, were not exempt from war, drugs, activism,
apathy, and severe identity crises. But that did not
necessarily mean that they had the insight — or the

right — to judge our ability to cope. After all, strengths and weaknesses are buried deep and take shape in the past. Character, inner resources are formed in the crucial early years.

As I drove across the prairies, longing for my children and grandchildren, straining to dredge up memories of my own childhood, I thought about the needs of young children in very personal terms. And I knew well that my unusual interest in the early years of development stemmed from my own past, all that I had had and all that I had missed as a little girl.

"The magic years are the years of early childhood," Selma Fraiberg has written. "By 'magic' I do not mean that the child lives in an enchanted world where all the deepest longings are satisfied. It is only in the minds of adults that childhood is a paradise, a time of innocence and serene joy. The memory of a Golden Age is a delusion for, ironically, none of us remembers this time at all. At best we carry with us a few dusty memories, a handful of blurred and distorted pictures which often cannot even tell us why they should be remembered. The first period of childhood . . . is submerged like a buried city . . ."

Submerged — but still there.

It is hard for me to know for certain what I remember and what I have been told about the early years of my own life. I was born on the night of November 25, 1921, quite unexpectedly, in my grandparents' farmhouse. My identical twin sister, Ila, weighing four pounds, arrived half an hour before I did and was put in a cotton-lined shoe box while relatives helped bring me into the world. Right before my birth, according to family legend, the doctor called for hot water and my dad rushed upstairs with a teacupful. Then I was born, weighing four ounces more than Ila, but with a respiratory problem that made it necessary for my grandparents and others to take turns warming me over a floor furnace burning feed corn while they worked to keep me alive.

My father's father had emigrated to South Dakota when he was eighteen from a farm near a town called Haugesund in southern Norway. My mother's family had pushed out to South Dakota from New England in the late 1880's. My dad, Earl Stegeberg, was a shy, withdrawn man who adored his wife, Marian, a sweet, independent woman with bright blue eyes and flaming cheeks; I thought my mother was beautiful, and so did everyone else. Both families objected to the marriage of my parents, but they had been sweethearts since childhood and love prevailed. I always thought that was romantic, particularly when I grew old enough to detect an ancient animosity between my maternal and paternal grandmothers.

Phyllis arrived when Ila and I were seven. I remember vaguely that Mother did not feel well one morning and we were sent away from the farm for the day. When we came home that evening, we had a baby sister, born in the downstairs bedroom with the help of relatives and a family doctor. It would have been a marvelous learning experience if we had been allowed to be part of the birth. Maybe we would have been nicer to Phyllis later on when she really needed us.

I do not remember when I first realized that I was an identical twin. My grandmother used to tell me that, before we could really talk, Ila and I carried on "conversations" with each other in gibberish that we seemed to comprehend but that made no sense to others. We were slight, mop-headed little girls, always dressed alike except on rare occasions when we were free to dress as we pleased and, inevitably, chose different outfits. I knew I was not the same person when I was with Ila as when I was alone. My shyness without her was acute. But we were unaware of the psychological implications of twinship until much later when parents of other twins asked, "How did you react to this?" or "How did you solve that?" It did not dawn on us that we were supposed to have problems with each other. Yet I know now that neither of us became whole, self-confident personalities until we made a painful break as young adult women.

In our childhood the rivalry must have been fierce. When Phyllis was learning to talk, we speculated endlessly about which one of us she loved most and therefore would call by name first. I should have known that it would be easier to say "Ila" than to say "Eleanor," but I was devastated when she did, and truly angry when the little toddler persisted in calling both of us "Ila" for a long time.

I do not think our twinship should have been encouraged as much as it was; our alikeness should not have been fostered. "Isn't it wonderful that Eleanor and Ila never say 'I' but always say 'we?'" we heard often.

Although it was wonderful always to have a play-mate, I staked out a secret retreat in an apple tree in the middle of the orchard near the house where I could be alone to sulk or to indulge in fantasy. I needed a sanctuary then as I need one now. I never worry when my own children want to be alone, and I encourage my grandson, Timmy, to curl up in his pri-vate place between the couch and the wall, where he goes to be quiet and tells me he is "hibernating." And when I visit day-care centers I always look to see if they have acknowledged a child's need to crawl under a table or to slip behind a cardboard wall or a clump of trees that can shield embarrassing tears.

Although memories of my South Dakota childhood are largely "blurred and distorted pictures" that never quite come into focus, I clearly remember prairies and farmlands, as my Mary Kay perceptively wrote in her poem, "where tall grasses grew," "shining soft colors of a setting sun," and, above all, "the blue open sky, like no other one."

We were wonderfully free to roam the farm, to gather wildflowers, or to play with the animals. Like most farm children we slid down haystacks and played hide-and-seek in the fragrant alfalfa and sweet clover fields. North of the barn was a grove of shade trees where Mother sometimes took us on picnics, building a fire with sticks on the bare ground to cook a hot noon meal if Dad was away as part of a threshing crew, helping neighbors to harvest the grain.

Mother was creative. The drudgery associated with motherhood — the work, loneliness, boredom — could be relieved if mothers thought of themselves as artists and their children as a medium. My mother did. Every day, every hour, as she hugged us and talked to us and sang to us, it was as though she were adding to our lives a touch of blue here, a touch of yellow there, a dab of black. She let us know by every action that it was her joy to care not only *for* us but *about* us, that we were as essential to her as she was to us. We felt valuable, able to accomplish wondrous, creative things ourselves, secure in the knowledge that we needed only to reach out to her to have our confidence shored up.

I think I remember best the summer she showed us how to create an imaginary playhouse at a certain spot in the orchard where the leafy plum and apple branches formed a thick protective roof. With her help we learned to mark out each room in the earth with twigs, tracing the walls deep in the soil around logs and boards and boxes and stones that served as cupboards, tables, and chairs. My own children were never so lucky. When they were old enough to play house, they had metal stoves and plastic furniture — unimaginative copies of the real thing that left little room for innovation — and radio and TV.

South Dakota summers were unbearable. Day after day scorching winds whipped across the plains. There were no hoses or sprinklers, and Mother and my sisters and I watered the trees and bushes by pail. Dad rigged up a metal box with circulating water in the corner of the stock tank to keep the milk sweet and the butter from melting. The stock tank was a huge, round wooden tub of water for the cows and horses to drink, and on blazing afternoons when Mother and Dad were in the fields Ila and I would sneak into the barnyard and slip over the splintery side into the deep cool water. It was a forbidden luxury. "You are not to go into the stock tank!" Dad would thunder before he left for the fields. But when the heat was insufferable, we simply risked his anger — my only memory of repeated childhood defiance of Dad. Sometimes we got away with it; sometimes not. It didn't take long to discover that the water stayed murky for a long time if we splashed around and stirred up the algae from the bottom of the tank.

During the winter we played in the big room near the storeroom, which had linoleum on the floor and was always kept very neat. We did not have many toys. I longed for a real doll from the Sears catalogue, but I contented myself by collecting bottles and dressing them as people or cutting out pictures for paper dolls from mail-order books.

Ila and I slept upstairs in the same room. In the winter to warm the bed we carried up with us an iron heated on the stove in the kitchen and wrapped in newspapers. Then we jumped in and covered up all but our noses in cold so bitter that a glass of water beside our bed would be frozen by morning.

Now and then curious details break into my consciousness: the heartbreak of a broken filament in the Aladdin lamp, which shed a brighter light for us to read by than the ordinary kerosene lamps; a rug beater we used when we hung our carpet from the living room on the clothesline; the Model T my grandfather traded in on a Model A; apprehension and wonder when we lighted real wax candles on a Christmas tree; Mother's sad acceptance when the spirea she planted around the front porch died, parched from the drought.

And there is a clearer, more burning memory of another trying day for Mother when she was the victim of an intrafamily argument. It happened late one afternoon. She was feeding the chickens; I was playing in the yard near some relatives who were waiting for her. As I casually eavesdropped on their conversation, I realized the women were plotting against her and I was stunned by the criticism and fascinated by the uncommon turn of events. I remember now that my urge was to rush to the chicken yard and warn Mother; yet something held me back. I think now my hesitancy was the natural ambivalence of childhood, that ever-changing, bittersweet, love-hate bond between parent and child. My mother had done something wrong? Impossible! Then why were her own relatives waiting to berate her? Before I could decide what to do about the drama unfolding before me, Mother came around the corner of the garage, smiling and waving, so pretty with her high coloring and her hair drawn back, reaching out to the people who waited to assail her with a tongue-lashing I shall never forget.

Later, miserable, I followed her to her room and crawled up beside her on the bed and we clung together. Even then I did not confess that I felt that everything — whatever "everything" was — had really been my own fault. After all, I knew that she was going to be hurt and I had done nothing about it. Instead, I had tested her vulnerability. I was desolate, too young to articulate my guilt, too ashamed to tell her about my frightening, conflicting feelings.

I think children often bear the burden of culpability for unhappy things they witness happening to others close to them — parents, brothers, sisters. It is a terrible load. I have one friend who threw up every time her older brother was punished; and another woman I know says that she is guilt-stricken whenever she remembers the time her father lost his job. We know so little about guilt, but I try to look for signs in my own children without losing the spontaneity of our relationship by analyzing them continually. I think a lot of confusing sorrow in later life could be avoided if parents were more alert to guilt-provoking behavior and discussed it openly at the time.

When Ila and I were old enough to go to school, we walked every day about one mile down the road to the schoolhouse, although there was a little barn there for those pupils who rode horses. For our first three grades it was the same one-room building, on a two-acre plot parceled out of a field, attended by both Mother and Dad. Then the old building was moved away and a newer one was brought from somewhere else to stand

on the same land, this one with an indoor bathroom.
I am glad that we were not sent to a large school
where we would have been segregated by age. We
learned much by observing older boys and girls and by
helping the younger ones, varying in number from
twelve to twenty-two. And then when we graduated —
the rural schools all held graduation ceremonies
together — everyone for miles around showed up, not
just the parents of pupils. Alfred Godfrey, a young
bachelor, taught all eight grades. At recess he carried
both Ila and me around the school yard on his shoulders, I suppose because the little Stegeberg twins
seemed fragile in the company of older, rough-and-
tumble farm boys, or perhaps because we were so
openly delighted to swing around the yard high up
above the others. The simplest events stirred excitement: a box social with special lunches packed in decorated boxes to be sold to the highest bidder; a visit
from the county superintendent of schools, or the
county nurse, or a parent.

Every afternoon Laddie, our collie, clairvoyant about
our plans to come straight home from school or to stop
off at Grandpa and Grandma Stegeberg's for cookies,
met us exactly halfway, either on the road or in the
field adjoining the farms. When there were blizzards,
Dad picked us up in the horse-drawn sled, which
wasn't so much fun as sliding over the frozen snow-
drifts blown into mountainous foothills in the roadbed
by icy prairie winds. That was play for us. When we
got home, there was always work, chores that had been

given to us as soon as we were old enough to share the burdens, as well as the benefits, of living in those days. Ours was a diversified farm. The crops were primarily feed grains, corn, barley, oats, a little wheat, some hay for the docile old work animals, but mostly grains to feed Dad's one cash crop, the hogs. Pigs were our sole source of income, except for the little bit that Mother saved for the household by selling chickens and eggs. Almost everything we ate came from a huge vegetable garden that Ila and I were paid a few pennies to weed. I hated to weed, but pennies and nickels meant a great deal then. Today nothing renews my spirit more than weeding my garden, working among roses and peonies, or eating vegetables so fresh that I think I can smell the dust in our big garden on the farm.

Dad also paid us a penny for every hundred sunflowers we dug out of the grain fields, but it was unthinkable to take money for gathering wood for the kitchen stove, feeding the chickens, turning the eggs every twenty-four hours during hatching season, and bringing the cows home for milking.

Fetching the cows from the pasture west of the house every evening, slowly heading home with the sunset behind me, provided important contemplative time. I noticed early that each cow had a distinct personality; some had leadership qualities; others always brought up the rear. I grew fond of a big, lazy cow at the end of the line and would rest my head on her ample, slow-moving body as we wended our way down the cow path. Those were hours when I first started thinking about the vast differences in animals and in people, about the wonder of individuality, perhaps with more intensity than a child who did not live with a mirror image.

We were seldom sick. In the spring and summer most of us had scuffed-up feet — it was an honor to be the first to go barefoot — and once after I jumped off the porch onto a board studded with rusty nails, the doctor warned against blood poisoning and Mother and Dad drove me seventeen miles every day to have the wound treated. It is a strong memory, not of pain, but of going so far away from home and of being carried. Years later, just before my third child, Teresa, was born, I remembered with adult longing those days when I was cuddled and cared for in strong, protecting arms.

It was inconceivable to me that any one of us, particularly my warm, lovely mother, might die. I think now she was a victim of the depression because she had to work so hard. She was only thirty-four when she died, a ruddy-cheeked woman with clear blue eyes, who sometimes played little songs on the upright piano in the living room, or tie-dyed pretty scarves and table-cloths, or lacquered brilliant bottles with scraps of bright paper lining from Christmas-card envelopes. But she was frail, and she died from surgery to relieve her of pain resulting from the births of Phyllis, Ila, and me.

By the age of eleven, when Mother died, I had seen death only once. When we were tiny little girls, Ila and I had set aside a pet cemetery in the corner of the yard between three lilac trees where we buried chickens, birds, even the wee field mice we found dead around the farm. But I had never sensed the finality of death until a newborn kitten died from distemper while I was holding it in my lap, stroking it, willing it to live. I recall that I cried because the cat was so sick and that my tears glistened on the animal's white fur. Then it shuddered and died in my hands. I wanted to go to Mother and talk about what had really happened, but I did not; later I read a frighteningly detailed description of death in an Andersen fairy tale that mentioned the Bible passage about "dust to dust" and I began to form my own fantastic conception of dying, based quite understandably on negating the whole thing.

When Mother told me she was going to go thirty miles away from home to a real hospital, I knew something was terribly wrong. I will never forget my apprehension. Or that I laughed. I think I was suffering too much to cry, but I have never forgotten that I laughed, and that Ila laughed, and Mother did not say anything to help us understand that laughter in a time like that can be an expression of grief.

A few days later, when Dad took us to the hospital to see her — she had gone to the Mitchell hospital because it was less expensive than the Mayo Clinic in Rochester — a nurse met us on the steps and I knew Mother was dead. But by the time I had taken a few steps to her deathbed, I had rejected the whole idea of her death.

I know now how serious it was for me to refuse to acknowledge my mother's death when I was eleven years old. In my mind even the services for her were being held for another person. I remember looking around the funeral parlor at cousins in tears and thinking to myself, "Why are they crying? My mother is not dead." I knew it was true, yet I knew with equal certainty that it was not.

The family did not pay much attention to me or to my sisters. I think they assumed that we were not suffering much because we were very young and probably insensitive to the dimension of the tragedy. Dad quickly usurped the position of chief mourner in the family; all attention was turned toward him; it was his loss of a beautiful young wife that was everybody's concern.

For many weeks I rejected reality. I was a child in crisis without the slightest idea of how to cope. One evening there was a long-distance telephone call from Mitchell — any phone call to the farm was special, but long distance always meant something of great importance — and I was sure that the call was from Mother, asking us to come to the hospital to bring her home.

I do not blame anyone for that childhood trauma. Our family and friends simply did not understand that Ila and Phyllis and I should not have been so excluded from sharing the pain of Mother's death; our confusion, that meld of sorrow, guilt, and anger that all children feel when a person abandons them, should not have been minimized. "A child should not be deprived of his right to grieve and to mourn," Dr. Haim Ginott wrote. "He should be free to feel sorry in the loss of someone loved. The child's humanity is deepened, his character ennobled, when he can lament the end of life and love."

"The end of life and love" is more than children can handle alone. And I can attest that if a youngster is not helped to accept death, is not supported through the ultimate crisis, it can cause far-reaching, lifelong problems.

Chapter III

"Working Hands"

As YEARS PASS, I am more and more impressed by the farmer's philosophy of life. Surely there are few greater virtues than perseverance. I grew up among people who never lost hope for a tomorrow when the rains would come, the winds would die away, the crops would flourish, the prices would be right, and the drought and depression would be over. In those days in the thirties there was always anxiety about the present, but faith in the future. Life was rugged, but it was an adventurous time to be alive.

The dust storms, for example, came upon us like the end of the world and laid waste the South Dakota farms all around. I learned to watch for the storms with Dad, and to this day I think I know when there is danger in a cloud formation. The first bad storm I

remember was terrifying. We were driving down a
country road when a strange, dark cloud rose along
the western horizon, billowing and churning as it
climbed higher and higher into the sky. I knew my
unemotional father was alarmed when he turned for
the farm, driving as fast as possible at thirty-five miles
an hour. By the time we reached home the sun was
completely shrouded and it was so dark that we had to
light the kerosene lamps to see. The wind howled for
hours. Dust seeped through the cracks around the
windows and doors and permeated everything. By the
next morning the sun was blazing again in a clear, un-
polluted sky, but our tender young grain had been
ravished and the crop was gone for the year.

It happened again and again: winds whipped over
the fields, stripped the grain and corn; then the thistles
rolled across the prairie and piled up against the
fences, trapping and packing the dust until little hill-
ocks were formed, across which the cattle and horses
and sheep wandered from one farm to the next. I
used to think that was nature's way of warning us not
to build fences.

Studies show that the dust bowl of the plains was really created back in World War I when farmers were
encouraged to produce in ever-increasing quantities to
feed the Western world. Land that nature had meant
for grazing was plowed. Then the drought years
came, the rains ceased to fall, the grasses stopped
growing, and the winds sucked up and blew away the
loose, fertile topsoil. Some neighbors fought the ero-

sion by terracing their land; others started strip farming and alternated corn with a ground cover; most planted shelter belts. But the rich topsoil had been dissipated, and what little earth was left needed to be fertilized with nutrients before anything could grow — and we could not buy commercial fertilizer then.

There were ruinous hailstorms too, but it was the grasshoppers I dreaded most. They came in frightening swarms and there was no way to fight them. Many farmers planted milo around the edges of the cornfields, hoping to divert the insects from the sweet new corn in the center of the fields. Others tried poisons. Dad was so desperate that he hired us to catch them by hand and paid us a cent for every twenty-five. Those were hard-earned pennies. The loathsome creatures were hard to snatch, and they left ugly brown stains on our hands.

Frequently anthrax wiped out a herd of cattle or several milk cows. The death of even one cow was a terrible loss. Cholera was prevalent among the livestock in the area, and we worried endlessly about losing a crop of spring or fall pigs. Those hogs were our real livelihood. So much depended on them, yet it was sheer chance to know when to sell, and we all engaged in the guesswork. Evening after evening Dad sat in front of the radio and analyzed the market report, listening carefully to the solemn recitation of figures. Then there was heart-stopping anxiety when he made a decision to sell. Tomorrow the price might go up and he would lose a few precious dollars. Or maybe the mar-

---

ket would go down and our funds would drop dangerously lower. In those days there were no extensive reports on scarcity or abundance. It was all a game of poker.

I still carry a trace of bitterness about poverty, not because being poor is hard, but because the poor are almost always victims of circumstances beyond their control. Their economic fate is in somebody else's hands. It is not ennobling to struggle for survival in a slum, just as it was not ennobling for my father and grandfather to scratch out a living on land rendered barren. The poor have few choices in life. About all they can do is persevere. But it seems to me that it is easier for a poor person to have hope when there is sun and sky above, when nature's mysterious, ever-changing rhythms are in full force, when there are endless, open plains as far as the eye can see, contributing to the illusion that everything seems possible and nothing is finite.

The summer after Mother died was a particularly bad one and Dad went away for several months to work near Watertown at a Veterans Conservation Camp. Farming was hopeless and, besides, he was lost and alone without Mother. Ila and Phyllis and I took turns staying with different grandparents. It was a dreadful time. I longed to stay put and was always overcome by a horrible, sinking feeling when it was time to pack up my few things and move on from one place to the next. Security, continuity, to know what

was expected of me and by whom — I needed that
kind of roots. Even today I have fleeting pangs of anxiety when I leave where I am to go to someplace else. I
can describe it only as a vague sense of loss of place. I
often wonder if my own children and grandchildren,
who have been moved time after time, like so many
other youngsters in our mobile society, aren't beginning to pay for it. It may be that today's children, who
pack up their roots with their other belongings, have
inherited not the dread of moving on but the fear of
staying put. Perhaps that accounts for a prevalent
longing to be involved, but a hesitancy to make deep
commitments.

We were all glad when Dad came home again. Ila
and I, twelve years old, took over as housekeepers for
him and as surrogate mothers for Phyllis. She says
now that she grew up thinking she was a brat because
Ila and I treated her as one. Her memories are poignant: times when Ila and I walked off to school without her, leaving her so desolate that she wanted to
die — in a spot where we would find her on our way
home; one day when Dad took the gun out to shoot a
favorite horse and I turned up the radio and made everybody sing until we mistakenly thought it was over,
stopped making noise, and then heard the shot; times
when she figured that Ila and I were prettier and
smarter because those who had lived with Mother
longer must have been better persons. I just remember that we used her shamefully by sending her to
sound out Dad when we were afraid to approach him.

We intuitively felt a need to assuage his grief, to lift the pall that hovered over the house. In our childish conspiracy to fill the void left by Mother, my twin sister and I grew closer; we shared responsibilities, shared joys, shared everything. If trouble brewed, we turned to each other, seldom to Dad, and only occasionally to our remarkable pioneer grandparents who rallied from both sides of the family to teach us how to manage the more arduous chores essential to keep the farm going.

I am proud of the Norwegian ancestors of my Father. A distant relative, Elsie Hansen, has traced them back to the year 1270. There is a family legend that my great-great-grandfather built a small fortune out of a silver dollar he received for being polite to a wealthy gentleman. Certainly none of that money crossed the ocean two generations later with my grandfather, Oman Martin Stegeberg.

What I remember clearly is that Grandpa Stegeberg was like David taking on Goliath in defending Mother against the rest of my father's family. I never did ascertain why my grandmothers disliked each other so intensely, but they did, and as far back as I can remember, Mother, both alive and dead, was the pawn on their chessboard. Grandpa made it clear that he truly loved Mother; therefore I loved him.

He was a troubled man. Making ends meet, holding on to what little he had, these constant worries were tooled in the grain of his face. But his rare moments of abandonment were memorable. "Great Scot! Let's dance!" he would shout at a neighborhood party, and be first to swing his powerful, wiry little body around the room; or he might burst into a simple Norwegian song, one of several I did not then and still do not understand, but learned to sing by heart; and often he would throw back his head and let deep, splendid laughter roll out. He was not funny, ever, but he was a lot of fun.

His wife, my paternal grandmother, Josephine Olson Stegeberg, who had moved to South Dakota from Colorado with her Norwegian and Dutch parents, seemed far bigger than Grandpa. She was forbidding, to say the least. The devil in her life was dissatisfaction, to be exorcised by working like a demon. She called for perfection in everything — scrubbing, cooking, cleaning, and people.

Grandma Stegeberg taught me all I know, and a great deal I wish to forget, about laundry. She was fastidious about the laundry, even though it took us literally days of hard physical labor to produce crisp, white, sweet-smelling, absolutely faultless linen and wearing apparel.

We soaked the clothes overnight. Then early in the morning we gathered wood for a fire and heated water for the washing machine and for a huge oblong iron boiler and as many pots and pans as we could fit on top of the stove. Into the washing machine went the first load: dishtowels, pillowcases, sheets, hand towels, and all the least grimy odds and ends. The machine was operated by pushing a lever back and forth to agitate the clothes, and the wringer was turned by hand. After the wet wash rolled out of the wringer, it was rinsed at least twice in tubs of clear water carried in from outside and then boiled in the pans of soapy water on top of the stove for about half an hour; the wringer again; a warm rinse; the wringer again; and another rinse, cold this time because there would be no soap left to "set." The soap was made by Grandma with lard rendered at the time of the annual slaughtering when one pig was taken from the crop and butchered, the fat stripped away, melted, mixed with lye, hardened, and cut into chips. It was strong enough to take the skin off our hands.

Today, when I see a family clothesline strung with washing, I usually think of Grandma Stegeberg. She did not hang things on the clothesline helter-skelter; she created a tableau. It was unthinkable, for instance, for her to reach down into the bushel baskets and grab what was on top so that the overalls might land next to, say, the sheets. No, our laundry went where it was meant to go — into some mysterious, interlocking, master plan.

The ironing took longer. Again at dawn we garnered fuel for the stove, lots of it, enough to keep the irons hot for hours and hours. Grandma showed us how to sprinkle the night before, to roll things up as tightly as possible so they would stay damp, and to tuck the pieces carefully like sardines into bushel baskets. It often took more than a day to iron the hand-embroidered flatwork, sheets, pillowcases, towels; and the dresses, gathered, ruffled, tucked, and pleated; the work shirts and the endless little rolls of spotless linens that came out of the seemingly bottomless baskets.

Willa Cather once wrote: "The one education which amounts to anything is learning how to do something well, whether it is to make a bookcase or write a book. If I could get a carpenter to make me some good bookcases, I would have as much respect for him as I have for the people whose books I want to put on them. Making something well is the principal end of education. I wish we could go back, but I am afraid we are going to become more and more mechanical." I do not wish, as she did, that we could "go back." But I am sorry that my daughters did not have the chance to observe a farm woman who did well and proudly what had to be done.

Grandma Stegeberg was always a contradiction to me, particularly in those years when I was half a child, hungry for approval and affection, and half a woman, eager to learn and please. I used to think that false pride was the only reason for her impeccability: her sparkling house; her beautiful tending, mending, and patching; her fussy, meticulous habits. But now I am more forgiving. I think she was groping for ways to express herself. Her laundry and darning were her works of art. Her frail, impractical garden of baby's-breath, marigolds, peonies, delphinium, which would live one year and die the next, was the only color in her lusterless life. Her personality was spare — she doled out splinters of affection — because she was simply more comfortable with things than with people. And as far as her granddaughters were concerned, she saw her duty, and she did it.

My maternal grandparents were loving, but they were not around so much as Dad's family, who lived on the adjoining farm. Mother's family had settled near Woonsocket on farmland discovered by my great-grandfather, who reportedly found it on a trip by boat down the James River — the one I tell people is the "longest unnavigable river in the world." My mother's mother, Edna Wright Payne Young, was widowed before I was born, and her second husband, Richard Young, whom we called Grandpa Dick, was our step-grandfather. He was an uncomplaining, pleasant man, who talked to horses and teased little girls. Phyllis remembers that he had a beautiful, bushy mustache that she used to stroke. One night when he appeared, it was gone. "What happened, Grandpa Dick?" she cried in alarm. "The wind blew it away," he replied. Phyllis says now that she was heartbroken and got up early the next morning to comb the yard for the beloved handlebars. My sisters and I agree that nothing seemed very wrong when we were with Grandpa Dick.

Grandmother Young was a storybook grandmother with snow-white hair. She gave all of us limitless, unconditional affection in spite of the long-standing family tensions. Grandmother was at Mother's bedside before she died and took very seriously her daughter's

last words, "Take care of my boy and my babies." She
knew who she was and where she was going — she
even walked that way — and she demonstrated her
pride in us with equal purposefulness.

Her house was always in an incredible clutter —
family pictures, books, flowers from the garden and
fields, where she spent most of her time — and it
smelled of green apple pie and bread pudding. She
could make anything taste delicious, and tried to teach
me how to stretch food without sacrificing natural fla-
vor. When she ironed, it was not a two-day produc-
tion, but a few hours here and there of pressing things
adequately — but just — her shirts were a horror — on
a straight board supported by two chairs. Long after I
was married, I sent her a real ironing board. She
loved it and immediately propped it atop two chairs exactly as she had always done.

Until the day she died, I could count on Grandmother Young for advice and for approval. She
thought her granddaughters were smart and pretty
and good. I remember complaining to her that I was
ashamed of my ugly hands. "Just be thankful, dear,"
she said then, and many times thereafter. "Those are
working hands. They are hands that can *do* something."

On one of my last visits to her modest little house in
Woonsocket, where she moved to spend her later
years, she told me she felt she had lived three full lives
as a mother, a grandmother, and the great-grand-
mother of twenty-four. Most of us do not really live

one life to the fullest. I thought about her when I heard the apocryphal story about the old farmer who rejected a book on modern farming techniques by telling the salesman, "I don't farm half as good as I know how already." Not Grandmother Young! She felt she had lived as well as she knew how, and she loved life right up to the end. I remember visiting her shortly before she died. While I was there, two old farmers dropped in for lunch. The three aged South Dakotans were old, old friends, all in their eighties, and deaf as posts. They had known one another for more than fifty years, and they were overjoyed to be together and to share a meal. It was a happy, satisfying scene to carry away in my mind: Grandmother, as flushed as if she had been square-dancing, and the two elderly gentlemen reminiscing about harder days, teasing one another about timeworn secrets, and bickering playfully, all at the top of their lungs.

My grandparents played a large part in my young life, and I know Ila, Phyllis, and I added much to theirs. Generations need one another. The futurist Robert Theobold told me not long ago that he thought one of the worst things we are doing in America is putting people into the "sun cities" where they are isolated from the young. It is bad for them and it is bad for society. The role of the parent, often an active and explosive one, is to help a child through confrontations in daily life; but grandparents have more time, patience, perspective, and can provide moderation and stability. Anthropologist Margaret Mead says they know best how to prepare the young for innovation and change and can show how the whole of life is lived to its conclusion. Pediatric psychologist Lee Salk, a friend of mine, says grandparents provide a child with understanding of the aging process, when grandmas and grandpas cannot easily get down on all fours and crawl around to play. I can still get down on the floor with Timmy, Matthew, and Kevin, but even if I could not, I can afford a few more minutes than their busy mothers can, to be sure they pick up their toys and hang up their clothes. I can give the little boys that indulgent second chance.

One of my good friends says that her sons call their grandparents "the rocks of Gibraltar." She is a city career woman, first divorced and then widowed, whose boys spend summers on a ranch with a grandmother who teaches them to care for the garden, the pets, to cook and barbecue, while the grandfather takes them hunting, fishing, camping, and lets them work in his shop. My friend and her parents have worked out a way of dealing with the boys that does not undermine the mother's authority or impose unrealistic demands on the grandparents, who have somewhat different rules. The boys can hardly wait to go to the ranch; and later they can hardly wait to go home. Nothing can replace the presence of their real father or their stepfather, but over the years they have developed a different type of relationship with loving adults with well-entrenched value systems, their mother is more

----

relaxed because she is less fearful about the void in their lives, and the grandparents are reinvigorated by the involvement with another generation.

My dream is a four-generation house for summers, holidays, and retreats from the real world. My fantasy home is for the McGoverns, the Meads, the Rowens, and the future families of Teresa, Mary Kay, and Steve. It is built like a wheel that revolves around a place where our families can interact, but only if·they wish to leave their own private quarters, which they will have designed, decorated, and furnished. I have been told that it is old-fashioned of me to want to keep my children so close. But I would not have this dream if I had not decided long ago that a family should be a flexible arrangement, a system offering a harbor for each member, allowing him to feel free to move out and back without recrimination or rejection or loss of contact. I am talking about a welcome place.

I think now that even if I had been raised by two parents in an environment with minimal stress, my grandparents would have influenced me almost as much as they did. Grandma and Grandpa Stegeberg taught me something valuable about work, and Grandmother Young and Grandpa Dick demonstrated the importance of love and trust. Now, from a different vantage point, I find grandparenthood an unexpectedly satisfying period in my life. I know my grandchildren need me. I need them.

Dad had left the parenting to Mother and, after she died, he never seemed to know quite what to do when he was left alone with Ila, Phyllis, and me. Even though he worked nearby and was always around the house, I felt self-conscious with him and suspected for years that he blamed us for Mother's early death. I know now that he tried to be a good father. He cared for us in an awkward, bumbling way, but we did not appreciate that. Our main concern was to compensate for being an added burden.

When I think of Dad, I see the color brown — his hair, his skin; he was always brown from farming in the sun. But his eyes were blue, not the faded eyes of so many men of the soil, but changeable like those of a person engrossed in thought. He was out of place on the farm, a mental man, not a physical one. I believed that he was the brightest self-educated man in South Dakota. And I also believe the average farmer in my state is better informed than most citizens because he has those long winters when the ground is frozen and life takes on a quieter, more thoughtful, and inward character. George says that my dad was a fascinating conversationalist, with deep "emotional crosscurrents," who was always probing for the meaning of things.

Hour after hour he read Spinoza, Hegel, Sweden-borg, anything he could get his hands on. He read aloud; he read to himself; he indulged in long mono-logues about what he was reading, insisting only that his girls be willing to sit with him and listen. During those long, tiring sessions, even though I ached until I wanted to cry, I developed a lifelong hunger for read-ing that has helped to fill huge gaps in my formal edu-cation.

In those early years our whole family used to take books near the one floor furnace and toast our feet and munch popcorn while we read. I still look for reading places where my feet will be warm, even if I have to pop them in an oven and turn on the heat. I have often heard George say that "after worrying about her family, what my wife does most is read." It has been one of the strongest influences of my life and, surprisingly, a controversial one. A few years ago, for example, my daughter Ann was quite hostile about the books I was reading about raising children. "You're always reading," she complained. "Why don't you trust your instincts when you don't know what to do?" My response was that we have to supplement our instincts with knowledge, that our instincts tell us what to do but not how or why. Furthermore, I told her, there are others who know more, and we should benefit and build on their experiences. I think now that Ann was just beginning to accept the idea that I was not all-knowing. But after she indicated that she was uneasy, I did start to read in private about parenthood, discipline, and behavior. After all, I rationalized, I would not have much confidence in a pilot who could not fly an airplane without constantly reading a book of instructions.

My father, more than any other human being, taught me that one must feel responsible for society. Concern for others, responsibility for others, caring for our fellow men — those were subjects our family talked about every Sunday afternoon within the context of friendly or boisterous family political brawls. In those hours Dad came out of his shell as if ideas were his blood and bone. Many arguments were really volatile, and I was captivated by the battle of the adult minds, the vociferous pushing and pulling. I think the Sunday custom started back in 1896 when my great-grandfather on Mother's side, Charles C. Wright, was elected to the South Dakota state senate on the Populist ticket, which some journalists remembered when describing George's 1972 effort as that of "another prairie populist."

My father never missed one of FDR's fireside chats. Eventually, after all of us had left home, he was elected Democratic county chairman. "He was a shy man and an introvert," recalls Joe Robbie, a former Democratic state chairman in South Dakota (and now a managing partner of the Miami Dolphins). "He came to my office every two weeks or so to talk about organizing the Democrats in Sanborn County. As we became better acquainted, I was able to draw him out more and more until he became quite animated for such a reserved person, particularly during the remarkable campaign conducted in South Dakota by President Harry Truman." I sometimes remind George that I was a good Democrat many, many years before he was.

Except for those rare times when flashes of political arbitrariness lighted up Dad's face, or when he read with excitement certain passages from the books of great philosophers, he was a quiet, remote man who worked silently and steadily in the fields and around the house, seemingly unconcerned about us; but Ila and I knew that there was another Earl Stegeberg beneath the surface. When it was time for us to go to high school, we were uneasy about leaving him and little Phyllis. He hated having us go; he worried that he had not prepared us for the problems and temptations that might confront us. He stewed a lot about boys. He knew that his props were being pulled out from beneath him for the second time and that he was losing not one, but two, home companions and substitute mates.

Only a few years ago my Mary Kay, our poet, wrote an awkward little verse I still carry in my wallet that describes the untenable position of an independent girl, proud of her family, clinging to the comfortable relationship it has provided and aware of her responsibility to it, yet eager to be trusted and released. She knew she had to leave home, but she wanted to be welcomed back. "You know me, and that is something special," she wrote. "I'll watch out for bad people and bright, flashing lights. For your sake, I'll be careful, when I must take flight." Times were less complicated when I left home to go to school, when I took flight, but I wish now I had tried harder to solace my dad the way Mary Kay tried to reassure me.

Chapter IV

The Swinging Gates

MARGARET MEAD SAYS that when the translucent walls of childhood no longer close in and a child moves out of his circumscribed world into adolescence, the paths leading out from the swinging gates are both entrancing and frightening. In my own adolescence I was much more entranced than afraid.

Although I try, it is still difficult for me to understand why adolescence is so painful. Mine was not. I have friends who say they wouldn't live through those mad, mercurial years again for anything in the world. But my teen-age years were happy and bursting with promise.

In 1936 we were both spared and restricted from making basic decisions about our lives or analyzing our best talents — one reason, I think, why many of my

----

generation are square pegs in round holes. Behind
the swinging gates there was a relatively clear path,
free from such diversions as the drug culture, a sexual
revolution, or value crises. No one I knew was searching, at least overtly, for the "identity" Erik Erikson says
is the merging of the inner person that we believe ourselves to be with the outer person perceived by the rest
of the world. What was *was*. I was Eleanor Stegeberg,
shy, worthy, I thought, and mentally pinching myself
because I was lucky enough to be able to go beyond the
eighth grade to high school. Many others were not.
Those days flash in my memory like an Andy Hardy
movie, cast with wholesome young men and scrubbed-
looking girls, striving in classes, competing in 4-H, and
fumbling through first dances and kisses. We were not
alienated, or apathetic, or angry. Each day was full.

In my recollection Woonsocket High is a spirited,
temperate scene. It was a structured school. We
marched up and down the steps to the command of a
bell. In contrast to the modern thrust of education,
developed to stimulate the desire to learn and the desire to grow, the idea then was to be taught, period.
Dean Francis Smith of Hampshire College told me he
calls this type of education, encountered by most of us,
"filling station" learning that pumps facts and figures
into the student. It seemed adequate at the time. I
never questioned the relevancy of what I studied or
how I was being taught. But neither do I remember
being particularly inspired by any subject or teacher.

Ila says now that she was bothered because I got better grades than she — we were always on the honor roll — but I was jealous because she was prettier and I had a conspicuously crooked front tooth and wore heavy-rimmed reading glasses. We never thought we looked alike. Each of us swore that the other had a straighter nose. But we enjoyed being twins — at least, I did. Dr. Helen Koch, who has studied twins and twin relations, says, "What are the ramifications of constant urging or pressuring of twins to be different, to be themselves, or conversely to be alike and devoted? May not an identical twin be expressing his individuality when he is most like his co-twin, since the two have identical genes?" She found great prestige value in being an identical twin — social support, more attention. From her research she concluded that sometimes being in the same class stimulated both to achieve more, but at other times the superiority of one child overpowered the other's self-confidence, and that school administrators should avoid rigid rules and decide each case separately after experimentation. I am glad we did not have to go through that. Being a twin was a good feeling. I always had a confidante, a friend, someone to share responsibilities, to ease loneliness. And I never dwelt on the uniqueness of our relationship.

Perhaps one reason I was not an anxious adolescent was that I simply did not have the time to be introspective. During our freshman year of high school, for instance, Ila and I got up early, helped Dad milk the cows, prepared the family breakfast, got Phyllis ready for school, drove eight miles to classes, and repeated a similar schedule at night, except in the dead of winter when snow blocked the roads and we stayed in a dormitory in the basement of Woonsocket High. For the rest of our high school years we worked for the Parsons and other families for room and board — scrubbing, washing, baby-sitting after school. On weekends we took turns going out to the farm to clean up for Dad. Somehow we managed school dances, basketball games, roller-skating parties, movies — and, especially, boys.

Not surprisingly, our first date was a double date and Ila and I were so bashful that we invited a *third* girl to go along with us. A few weeks later, at a school dance, I spent the evening hiding from an awesome junior boy, whom I wanted desperately to ask me to dance. I still consider it magic that he searched all over until he found me. But I remember the gregarious moments of my new life most vividly: the day Ila and I were chosen to be school cheerleaders; wearing to dances an unfamiliarly luxurious pinky-red angora sweater that Aunt Di knit for me, even though I knew the fluff would come off on my dancing partners; my first argument with a boy about politics; and learning to debate, which undoubtedly altered the course of my life.

South Dakota has always been a forensic state. George says, "If I had not gone out for debate, there is not a chance in the world that I would ever have come to the United States Senate. It was the one thing that I could do well. It really became the only instrument of personal and social power that I had." In my case I know I would have stayed on the outskirts of things as a political wife without those lessons that I learned in debating classes. Even though I always dread public speaking, I do it, and I am always glad. In adolescence, developing the poise and confidence to think on my feet helped to crack the protective armor of reserve and inhibition I had accrued in my relatively isolated childhood. Of course, debating was easier for me because I had my twin by my side.

We must have been a sight: two eager farm girls, not quite five feet tall, carbon copies of each other, echoing our arguments with double zeal, even though the best forensic practice is to pick a team whose partners have markedly different personalities. I hate to think now that the coach may have thought we were cute, for we were very serious and researched for the debating season as though we were preparing a legal brief for the Supreme Court, reading, reading, reading, carefully building a card file with back-up data from magazines and books we sometimes tracked down from other parts of the country.

I would have been too nervous to debate George McGovern if I had known about it in advance. His reputation as a skilled polemicist, as a star debater of Mitchell High, had already been established, and the other member of the Mitchell team, Matt Smith, was an expansive, articulate young man. But the day Woonsocket High met Mitchell High to argue the question:

"Resolved: That Britain and the United States should form a permanent alliance," a contemporary issue stemming from the ominous build-up of Nazi strength in Europe, Ila and I had been picked to argue the negative. When I found myself on that platform with George in our first confrontation, it was much too late to flee.

I have always thought it curious that I don't remember George's exposition. Matt, on the other hand, made a lasting impression by punching the air and, in a booming voice, calculating that an alliance between the United States and Great Britain would generate what he called "a *preponderance* of power, a *preponderance* of power." When it was our turn, Ila and I asserted that the two countries did not need a permanent arrangement because a preponderance of power already existed without a formal treaty arrangement. We won. Afterward Matt punched the air some more and said, "I can't believe it, I can't believe it," and there was a rumor that George thought the Stegeberg twins had flirted with the judge. That was the only formal debate with George that I ever won, but through the years we have been nourished by arguing our different points of view. We really do listen to each other.

Today forensics, music, drama, athletics — those outside activities so important in helping young people to discover inner strengths and weaknesses — have become too specialized and professional. In the large suburban schools that my own children attended off and on, a student had to be truly gifted to be in the class play, highly proficient to have a place in the band or orchestra, or outstandingly attractive to represent the school in public events, whether as homecoming queen or in poetry contests or swimming meets. I believe that just *doing*, just investing the time and energy to participate in a new endeavor, is worthwhile to an individual who does not know how much if any talent he has because he has never had the chance or the audacity to try it out.

According to educator James S. Coleman, "schooling, as we know it . . . is not giving all the necessary opportunities for becoming adult." He believes that high schools particularly must create opportunities for young people to assume real responsibility and to become adults in all ways, not merely intellective ones. Alvin Toffler, author of *Future Shock,* suggests that high schools offer apprenticeship programs and that business and industry help train the young for today. I believe in going much further. If we interpret the word "education" in its broadest sense, as many communities are already doing, our schools can be exciting hubs of activity, not only learning centers but places where young and old can find broad social and cultural services, such as family counseling that sweeps from early childhood through the later years. After all, generations must work and play and learn together in day-to-day living, and educational systems should provide new and richer relationships for us by showing us how.

When I graduated from Woonsocket High, my confidence and competitive instincts were healthy enough

----

for me to be disappointed that I was not valedictorian, but only salutatorian. On graduation day I frantically rewrote my speech at the last minute so that Dad would be proud of me anyway. Ila and I had been worrying about him. That year both baccalaureate and graduation exercises were to be held, and there was great excitement about what everybody would wear to each occasion. We simply could not ask Dad to spend money for four complete outfits. Night after night we quietly pored over the Sears catalogue and finally settled on a blue dress for baccalaureate night. Then we screwed up our courage and asked Dad if he could afford to buy two of them. But for the graduation ceremony we wore white sharkskin suits, two years old and shiny, and it did not bother us at all.

We knew that Dad had saved only $100 for each of us to go to college, but we applied to several institutions more on the strength of desire than from a belief that we could ever work things out financially. Yet when the days seemed darkest, we were unexpectedly recruited to join the freshman class of Dakota Wesleyan University with the promise of secretarial jobs at twenty-five cents an hour with the college's dean, Dr. Matthew Smith, Sr., and its treasurer, Harmon Brown.

In the fall Ila and I moved into the girls' dormitory in an old Sioux Falls granite building on campus. Our room was large by today's standards, with a northern exposure looking out on a balcony where some girls sneaked out for cigarettes. I had never seen a woman smoke before. Nor had I realized that promiscuity would be discussed openly. Along with my determination to heed Dad's admonition against sexual liberties, I remember feeling a curious envy of girls who seemed so sophisticated. In fact, I never even allowed a boy to kiss me good-night unless I was certain that he wanted to kiss Eleanor Stegeberg and not just a girl. About that time Grandmother Young, back from a trip, told me that she had met two young men from New Orleans who told her they *assumed* the girls they took out would kiss them good-night. She was indignant and so was I. (Neither of us could have forecast that a contemporary of my children would be quoted in a magazine as saying, "There's no more of this good-night-kiss-on-the-first-date routine. When I take a girl out for the evening, I expect it to be an all-night affair, and nine times out of ten that's what it is.")

There is no question about it, when I first started dating George, I was naive. I had seen him on campus often. Once he was Ila's partner for a ladies' choice at a skating party. Another time in the library he unsuccessfully urged us to join the college debating team. At some point during the year he and I tied by getting 98 out of a possible score of 100 on a *Time* magazine current-events quiz, and George says now that he then made a mental note to get to know me better. Then on one especially balmy April day, toward the end of our freshman year, I looked up from my desk in the dean's office and saw George at the door, tentatively moving toward me, first lingering around the regis-

trar's counter, then near Dean Smith's door, and, finally, directly over me. I was truly stunned. He was
the formidable debating rival, the handsome campus
leader, the brain; but he was also inviting me to go with
him to the senior play.

It was a dreamy spring. I had never known anything like it before. My only concern was that George
might not care so much as I. Then on a beautiful clear
afternoon he urged me to skip class with him and as we
strolled slowly down the street south of campus, he
reached down and took my hand. I had my answer.
A clasping of hands meant everything then.

Chapter V

Breaking Away

GRANDMA STEGEBERG'S REACTION was sententious: "I think it's wrong for you to marry and leave Ila, when she has given up nursing school to come back home."

George's mother was resigned: "Well, at least George won't be all alone when he's away from home."

My father's opposition was total: "It's ridiculous! No! I will not come to the wedding!"

We had planned to be sensible. We were not going to settle down until World War II was over and George, who had volunteered for the Army Air Corps, was home again and had his degrees and a teaching job. But after a few months in basic training he wrote from San Antonio and asked me to marry him as soon as possible. No one, not even Dad, was going to stand in my way.

Actually, Dad liked George and said that he was glad we were engaged. They had been influencing each other since the first night they met, when I left for a party without George, who was unforgivably late, and the two sat down and talked about politics and Dad's views about chastity until I came home. Dad knew that someday I would marry George, but he didn't want it to be now. I think he would have preferred keeping it always in the future. He felt that way about all three of his girls. How hard it was for me to defy him! Except for swimming in the stock tank, I had never really done it before.

Grandma Stegeberg's concern about Ila was more understandable. My twin sister and I had been disturbed by our inevitable separation as we moved into different phases of our lives. Yet neither of us had been prepared for the wrench. It happened when there was no more money for a second year at college and I went to work as a legal secretary, while Ila started nursing school in Rochester, Minnesota. We did not necessarily miss the other's physical presence; yet for a brief period of time our everyday lives were invaded by unsettling moods and feelings: once I was unable to utter a word to two very good friends; at other times I was nearly ill from self-consciousness; and both of us suffered from a numbing, dead-end inadequacy we had never felt before. Our self-confidence had been as a pair, and the cleaving of our twinship left us only half human beings with the other half to be rebuilt. Our psychic split was easier for me, near home, family, and George; but Ila was cut off completely. "I was miserable," she says, "and I made everyone else miserable with my letters. I did not know how to function as a person all alone. And so I had to go home."

I can understand why Grandma Stegeberg thought that we could and should cling to our old relationship. People in her circle were not subjective. No one talked about the need to relinquish things in our lives when they no longer serve us; no one read magazine articles or saw television plays demonstrating that people should let go of childhood in order to be adults; no one discussed what was mature and what was not. When Ila and I were forced by circumstances to learn to be truly self-reliant, we knew that it was wholesome. But we were amazed that our struggle for self-sufficiency was being exploited as a weapon to fight my plans.

Predictably, Grandmother Young was steadfast in her belief that whatever I did would be right. She was as serene as ever. But it was unnerving to me to ignore Dad's vehement objections and to accept the McGoverns' lukewarm enthusiasm. I felt as though I were romping through a glorious, sun-struck meadow with both feet weighted down with bricks.

The wedding plans unfolded cheerlessly. Aunt Blanche Payne and George's mother planned bridal showers; Aunt Diantha Cosio, my only other real supporter, rounded up cousins to serve as ushers and neighbors and relatives to prepare a simple wedding lunch; Ila and I bought a dress for her, which neither of us liked, and some sheer, azure blue wool for me, which Mrs. Callihan in Woonsocket made into a two-piece wedding outfit (I did not have a trousseau because I had spent what little I had saved on sixteen dollars a week to have the dentist straighten my front tooth); I bought two inexpensive gold wedding bands, one for George and one for me, because we could not afford to buy the ring to match my little diamond; George's father, a Wesleyan Methodist minister, agreed to perform the rites in the small, pretty Methodist Church in Woonsocket on Halloween Sunday, October 31, 1943; and Dad, bitterly resisting the whole idea, insisted that he would not attend the ceremony at all.

I did not give up my job in the legal offices until the day before the wedding, leaving crucial last-minute errands to be done on Saturday afternoon, by which time I was so worn out I had doubts about the whole thing. Then I waited at the train station, fearfully, until George arrived, not as planned, but three trains and four hours later, in fact, too late to get the marriage license.

But the next day we were married in a very simple ceremony. Harvey Asper, register of deeds, met us at the church with the big, heavy Book of Marriages — and a marriage license. In attendance were dear relatives and good friends, bearing no visible traces of animosity or disapproval, and joining us at the reception in the church basement. Everything was perfect.

Even my father — my disappointed, uncommunicative, beloved dad — showed up without explanation to give me away.

Harry Emerson Fosdick once wrote, "War's tragedy is that it uses man's best — his skill, his courage, his self-sacrifice — to do man's worst." I thought of those words many times during the war in Vietnam, but back in World War II many Americans thought we were using man's best to do man's best. We did not like war, but we were proud of America and never questioned giving — giving up our young men, giving up our national treasure, giving up our affluent way of life. To fight for democracy, to lose our lives for freedom, that was the noble and decent thing to do. We never wondered then, as I do now, why world leaders with vision and a sense of history seemed powerless to deal with Hitler, Mussolini, Tojo. We never spent much time analyzing whether the war could have been *prevented* if America had been less passive, less self-satisfied with dominance in the world arena.

It is hard today for our five children to accept the fact that, during the months George was in training at home and in combat overseas, we assumed without question that it was right. "What is worth dying for?" our nineteen-year-old Steve asked one night in a family discussion about Vietnam. "That's the wrong question," Sue said. "It's easy to say we would *die* for a cause, but should we *kill* for one?"

George has said this about World War II: "It seemed

to me that what I was doing was central to the defense of Western civilization."

I thought so too, and I was proud of him.

I loved being a cadet wife. George does not think our first few months were like a marriage and says they were more like "a series of dates under enormous pressure — bittersweet." But for me it was great adventure just to be near him and to leave Woonsocket for places with names like Muskogee, Pampa, Liberal, Lincoln, Mountain Home.

Sometimes I think that, in moving from base to base while George was learning to be a pilot, we spent the most hours in the Kansas City Union Station, still a sentimental place for us. We changed trains there the day after the wedding, exhausted, stiff from sitting on our luggage in the aisle of a hot, crowded, airless coach. The cavernous depot was teeming with men in uniform and their wives and families. We were eager to plunge in and feel a part of it, and when we could not find a place to check our suitcases, simply dropped them on the floor and walked away, hand in hand. We felt reckless and we were. While we were gone everything we owned was stolen.

In Muskogee, Oklahoma, I lived on $50 a month in a rented room in a private home — I kept milk and cheese in my closet — and visited George at Hatbox Field once a week. For our first Christmas we gave each other letters, put under a tiny tree. In our family we still give letters, or poems, or notes on special occasions. Sometimes this opens up great avenues of

communication between us. I would rather have
words written just for me than any gift money can buy.
One year Steve composed a song for me on my birthday; another year Mary wrote a Christmas letter and
promised to quit smoking; and another, Sue put in
words how much more she appreciated me as a mother
after she had had a child of her own.

At each new base the cadet wives drew together,
some picking up little jobs, as I did, others drifting
aimlessly through the transient days and nights. I had
never before had an opportunity to share those inte-
rior relationships women can have with one another,
with the exception of close times with my own sisters.
We seldom mentioned the war. In fact, one night we
froze out a young wife who said she suddenly sensed
that "something's happened to Don." We were not
sympathetic. She had violated our unspoken code.

George was commissioned a Second Lieutenant in
the U.S. Army Air Corps in Pampa, Texas, a spot so
dusty that even the residents warned us not to judge
the whole state of Texas by the little town. The night
before graduation there was a ball for Class 44-D in a
decorated auditorium filled with couples dancing to
soft, romantic Tommy Dorsey songs. Afterward I
gave George an identification bracelet, an unimaginative graduation gift, I think symbolic for me that I was
Lieutenant McGovern's wife. He must have had a similar need to reinforce our vows. Unexpectedly, shyly,
that night he gave me a little box — he had sent back
to Dahles Jewelry Store in Mitchell for the gift. Inside

was the wedding band that matches my engagement ring. I wore both wedding rings the next day — and I have ever since. Dressed up in my best gold wool suit and a brown velvet hat I had made myself, I pinned the coveted shiny wings on George's uniform. I knew then that I was going to be afraid and lonely.

Now George was ready to fly the "big bird," a B-24, and to command a crew of men, some of them so much older than he that he grew a mustache (when he shaved it off he heard one say, "Hell, he isn't any older than I am"). How he looked was the least of his worries. There was something much worse. George hated to fly. He was afraid of taking off, landing, and every minute in between. But he was brought up in a strict family to believe in the Puritan ethic, to expect that with discipline, sacrifice, and hard work faith prevails and fear can be conquered; and he was raised in the era of Roosevelt's persuasive slogan, "The only thing we have to fear is fear itself." Indeed, fear was his major motivation for joining the air branch of the service. "I think if there's something you are particularly afraid to do — and there are no legitimate grounds for that fear — then it is all the more important that you go ahead and do it," he said years later, still able to recall the exact mission, the precise glorious moment, when he first realized that he had accomplished what he had set out to do and was no longer terrified.

A person is robbed of freedom if he lives in fear — freedom to grow, to change his environment, to become a whole person. He is imprisoned as truly as if he were in a cage. That is why I am interested in "outward-bound" type courses in schools today that teach young people the value of pushing to overcome the fearsome straw men that our minds create when we are devoid of confidence. When George was flying, he was not a victim of the what's-the-use attitude of some youths today; rather, I am sure that he thought it was good for his character to overcome his phobia. That is not easy to do alone and not every person can manage it. But for George it always seems to work, and throughout our life together he has helped me to stretch further, to face the bigger challenge, and to remember that we are all a bit better than we think we are. Like Robert Kennedy, who said, "Men are not made for safe havens," he believes that all life is a risk.

I was pregnant when George shipped overseas. Before he left, he took me home to Dad. It seemed the natural thing to do. Phyllis was in high school and Dad needed someone to help with the housework and I needed to work, which is always therapeutic for me. My father disapproved of my pregnancy. He thought having a baby was foolish for the exact reason that I was overjoyed — if George did not come back from the war, at least I would have his son or daughter. I suppose it was quite natural for Dad to want to spare me the possibility of single parenthood. It had been a formidable experience for him.

I worried and worked and worked and worried. I

did not speak of my fears to anyone, but I did not have
to, because by that time foreboding permeated the
house, the town, the country. I was haunted by the
memory of the night a plane had crashed while I was
in the base hospital at Mountain Home, Idaho, in the
early stages of my pregnancy. When I heard the
ghoulish sirens that signaled disaster, I ran out of my
room and begged an orderly to find out if George was
safe. He rushed away but never came back. Our wing
of the hospital was deserted. It was more than an hour
before I heard the door at the end of the hall and ran
out again, and there was George. After that, my imagination often slipped out of control.

Every evening I wrote to George and read Bible passages he had suggested before he left: "Yea, though I
walk through the valley of the shadow of death, I will
fear no evil: for thou art with me; thy rod and thy staff
they comfort me." "To every thing there is a season, and
a time to every purpose under the heaven . . . A time
to kill, and a time to heal . . . A time to weep, and a
time to laugh; a time to mourn, and a time to dance
. . . A time to get, and a time to lose . . . A time of
war, and a time of peace." And every morning I
waited to see if Cousin Milo, who worked at the post
office, would bring a letter that would tell me how
many of the required thirty-five missions were left for
George to fly. I first looked for the number of missions he had flown; then I would track back to read the
news, searching between the lines for clues about
where he was and what he was really doing. Grandpa

Stegeberg, who longed to go back to his fatherland again in his life, hoped the crew was flying at least near Norway. "Drop a note over Haugesund," the dear old man had said earnestly before George left. "They'll know who I am. They'll know."

It was an enigmatic period for me. I was a bride, but without a husband; pregnant, but not yet a mother; a daughter and housekeeper, yet unwilling to retrogress into that role completely. For the first time in my life I was openly furious with Dad. One afternoon when I thought he was unfair to Phyllis, I flew off the handle: "Oh, let her alone! She hasn't done anything wrong!" I snapped. Both he and I were absolutely astonished. In view of my past behavior such audacity was incredible. I remember my heart thumped madly and I felt quite faint. My dad looked intently at me, then grinned slowly, just a faint, poignant smile that I know now sanctioned the end of our father-and-daughter ties and the beginning of a comfortable adult-to-adult friendship. We liked each other much more after that.

I made up my mind early that I would urge my own children to express their honest emotions, no matter how ugly they might seem. In a family all the passions are put into play that are in the larger community, and that means that life cannot always be harmonious. In my view the members of a family need to be confident enough to express anger, jealousy, hurt, meanness, and know that such expression will not shut off love. I remember a particularly hostile time in my own family when the children were saying insolent things to me and I was sorry for myself. I asked a psychologist friend of mine, Bertha Stavrianos, what I should do. "Do they hate me?" I asked. "Can it be true there is no love there at all?" Her reply was enormously helpful. "Just the opposite, probably. Your children are sure enough of your love to reveal the way they feel. If they feared losing you, they would sublimate their feelings some other way. It is probably more positive than negative."

Just before Christmas George's father died suddenly. My mother-in-law was more grief-stricken and helpless than many widows, and I began dividing my time between Dad and her. I got along easily with all of the McGoverns. They accepted me. I always knew that Father McGovern had wished that George had married within the rigid, fundamentalist Wesleyan Methodist Church, but he was kind to me even though, according to his beliefs, I had been neither saved nor sanctified. We liked each other from the first time George took me home. That day I had decided not to offend my potential in-laws by wearing lipstick — as taboo for Wesleyan Methodists then as smoking, drinking, or dancing — but at the last minute put on my usual trace of color because I thought they should see me as I was.

Mother McGovern had a benevolent spirit. She was the kind of woman who reacted to the victorious headlines that there were thousands of German casualties at the Battle of the Bulge by crying, "Oh, dear, that means terrible grief in thousands of German homes!" Enemy or not — she saw the human tragedy. She always cut through to the goodness in people. I loved being with her, and was at her house when I went into labor with Ann.

The birth of our first child was a thirty-six-hour family affair at the Mitchell Methodist Episcopal Hospital. Ila, a technician in the lab, and George's sister Mildred, a nurse on the obstetrics ward, were in attendance in the delivery room, and Dad and Phyllis and Mother McGovern and a changing stream of relatives waited outside. I did not expect a difficult birth. My chief concern was that I had gained so little weight that I did not think the infant could weigh more than three pounds; the doctor predicted five pounds. When the baby was born weighing six pounds, twelve ounces, the word quickly spread through the hospital that the diminutive Mrs. McGovern had surely surprised the doctor by being "so round, so firm, so fully packed," a popular cigarette commercial in those days, now a family legend.

I could hardly convince myself that my new baby was not the little boy we had decided to name Joe after George's father, Joseph. Instead, they brought me a delicate, beautiful girl baby, an exquisite creature, every bit as lovely as my mother, for whom she would be named. I was jubilant.

Mother had been dead for thirteen years, yet I felt somehow, miraculously, her tiny namesake would help to make up for my loss. Then Dad came to see the baby. He told me that to be constantly reminded of

Mother would be almost more than he could bear. Once again, as had happened so often in the past, that peculiar combination of sadness and responsibility for his aloneness washed over me. And so I cabled George in Italy that his first daughter, Ann Marian McGovern, had entered the world.

In 1957 George took me to Italy and showed me where he and his crew had celebrated Ann's birth. I had visualized the officers' club, spacious, comfortable quarters with a fireplace, bars, and tables, filled with attractive young men in battle dress raising their glasses to toast Lieutenant McGovern's baby girl. In reality, the officers' club was an area about fourteen feet by thirty feet, that had since then been turned into a stable near the B-24 runway, a field now plowed into grain. I remember saying to George, "Well, here at least, since our first child was born, some swords have been turned into plowshares."

I might have grown resentful about Dad's disapproval of my pregnancy and his subsequent success in warding off painful emotion at my expense, but he fell in love with Ann and she changed his whole life. At first he would not touch her, but hovered over her as though he were keeping his eye on a jewel collection. "No, no, I could never do that." He shook his head when I urged him to pick her up. "She's so tiny, and I'm too awkward." One day I simply walked over and placed the baby in his arms. I could not believe what happened. My father threw back his head and a chuckle of joy bubbled out of him, the soft laughter flowing on and on, erasing the lines near his mouth that made him look so stern. I knew he had found someone who could make his years worth living. And from that moment on, Dad worried about Ann's diet, her sleeping habits, her shots, her temperature; he rocked her and he walked her; he agonized when she sniffled, and insisted that I move her out of the house when Phyllis came down with the measles. His life revolved around the hours he could be with her. And he gave her warmth that had been pent up inside him for years.

Once when it was time for a meal, Ann yelled at the top of her lungs, "Grandpa, come to 'upper!" Dad appeared instantly. "I'd go around the world in answer to that call," he said. Today Ann cannot understand why some people describe her grandfather as a cold man. He was more tender with her than anyone else in her early life. They gave valuable, uncompromising love to each other, grandfather and granddaughter, when each needed it.

When George came home from World War II, we met almost as strangers. Our letters had been full of romantic plans for the honeymoon we had never had. And we had salted away a little money to travel, to play, to get acquainted, and to live together as newly married lovers, free at last from the fear of death. It was unsettling to acknowledge that we would never have that period of abandon with each other. Instead, there were now three of us.

George has never said so, but I suspect that even though he worshiped little Ann, he must have felt at least temporarily cheated out of the relative freedom of being a couple instead of a family. Different kinds of bonds are established between people who love each other and must endure separation. But nothing, nothing can replace the sharing time that is lost. In 1973 I relived the ambivalence of our postwar reunion, when the prisoners of the Indochina conflict finally came home to strange wives, strange children, strange families, released into relationships irrevocably altered by unshared experiences.

Anne Morrow Lindbergh has written, "The 'veritable life' of our emotions and our relationships also is intermittent. When you love someone you do not love them all the time, in exactly the same way, from moment to moment. It is an impossibility. It is even a lie to pretend to. And yet this is exactly what most of us demand. We have so little faith in the ebb and flow of life, of love, of relationships. We leap at the flow of the tide and resist in terror its ebb. We are afraid it will never return. We insist on permanency, on duration, on continuity; when the only continuity possible, in life, as in love, is in growth, fluidity — in freedom, in the sense that the dancers are free, barely touching as they pass, but partners in the same pattern."

I had not read those words then, but I felt something similar. I knew we had both changed, that things were different. George was as idealistic as ever, but he was restless about his future. War had shocked him terribly. Night after night I was jolted out of sleep by his half-conscious cries — "The plane's on fire" or "The flak's getting heavy." Then we would hold each other and talk and talk. He could not stop questioning, quietly, urgently: Why war? Why war? It was months before he extinguished the mental images of B-24's in flying formation exploding in midair; or the "Dakota Queen," his beloved Liberator bomber, an old crate of an airplane that had to be guided by sheer physical force; or starving Italians digging in garbage cans in the olive grove outside his tent; or the empty bunk of Sam Adams, his navigator, who did not come back from a mission.

Those restless nights with his conscience were a prelude to a lengthy testing period for him. In the course of the next six years he finished college, preached in a small, lakeside Methodist parish, worked as a graduate teaching assistant in history at Northwestern University, earned his Ph.D., was a history professor at Dakota Wesleyan University, and finally gave it all up for politics. We moved nearly a dozen times in and out of South Dakota and Illinois, dragging along our burgeoning brood of babies to be fed, clothed, and sheltered. And with the exception of a few months — critical ones for me — they were the least hectic times in our marriage.

I was beginning to have confidence in my own ability. Be a minister's wife? The idea at first appalled me. But why? I would be me, no matter where I lived or what my husband did. Besides, I liked my life. It

took all of my resources to be a wife and mother. I
cannot remember being bored — exhausted, yes, but
never wondering what to do with my time. I had feelings of omnipotence. And I had my own private goals,
lofty ones: to be the world's best mother; to be supportive of George if he needed me; mainly, to be a significant person, somehow, no matter what I was doing.

In the long run George's brief attempt to embrace
the ministry — Mother McGovern said it was unsuc-
cessful because it had been an intellectual decision and
not "a calling" — was valuable precisely for its lesson
about the "intermittency" of goals. Robert Anson
wrote in a biography about George that he was following in his father's footsteps. "For a young man of his
background, home from the trauma of war, the ministry offered a natural refuge, a sort of emotional halfway house, a chance, as it were, to be in the world and
not really a part of it. The ministry represented famil-
iarity and comfort, much of the sort that he had enjoyed as a boy." But being a minister was not the same
as being a minister's son. Things, people change, and
George had. From that effort to devote our lives to
the church, both of us took something away that has
served us well and often: the courage to change our
minds. In 1972 this did not turn out to be a popular
principle.

It took flexibility simply to live the way we lived in
the academic world. In one old rooming house in
Evanston, for example, every time a neighbor sprayed
the swarming host of tenant cockroaches, another

neighbor was besieged, and every time a family moved away, all the other families swapped apartments in a sort of upward mobility shift. George fashioned bunk beds out of dresser drawers for little Ann and Susan. (Sue was born a year after Ann. I think I wanted her to have a twin relationship.) And we practiced fire drills on boards from under the beds that reached across the alley to the window of another building. Sometimes we subsisted for weeks on peanut butter, soup, and milk, budgeted out of an unreliable income made up of George's G.I. veteran's check, commissions he earned from selling Maico hearing aids, extra cash I contributed by sitting in a closet to type masters' theses and doctoral dissertations, plus a few pennies George collected by turning in empty soda bottles scrounged from around the apartment with a fellow graduate student from Mitchell, Bob Pennington, who had married my sister Ila.

Ila and Bob had been married right after the war in the same pretty little Woonsocket Methodist Church where George and I were wed. Later Phyllis married there too. Dad disapproved of all three marriages, and complained that each event was more elaborate than the last. He was right about that. Before Phyllis took her vows, I spent two months at home making formals for the bridal party, including a flower-girl dress for our beautiful, blue-eyed Sue, who interrupted the wedding ceremony when she toddled away from the altar and worked her way back up the aisles, laboriously replacing flower petals in her little basket.

It was comfortably clannish to be a student wife away from home, particularly with a twin sister nearby. And George and I had congenial friends at Northwestern, including history faculty members attracted to the minds of the ambitious, more mature veteran students. As a group the student historians and their professors have since been described as the "social activists" of that era, young men moved by their overview of war to believe that they could influence history if they were involved in it. Most were liberals opposed to Cold War policies; some, like George, were inspired briefly by Henry Wallace's vision of a world at peace. Many, also like George, chose topics for their graduate dissertations that had social significance — he started research on the Ludlow Massacre, a terrible Colorado coal strike in 1913. For all of them history seemed alive, meaningful, and a proper framework for maturing political philosophy. Years later, remembering the vital aura of potential that hung in the air those days, I turned to Walter Lippmann at a dinner party and asked, "Do we *learn* from history?" "We learn only one thing," he confirmed, "that people throughout history have reacted the same way to similar circumstances."

I was pregnant for the third time when I plunged into the doldrums. It came as a complete surprise. I was busy and happy. And George was relishing his graduate studies. I can see him now working over papers in the corner of our little living room, oblivious to the squeals of the little girls tumbling on the floor beside him, just as twenty-three years later he edited speeches on his campaign jet without heeding his grandson Matthew crawling under his feet. The girls were healthy and delightful, and I was looking forward to a third child. Then suddenly one day I was miserable. And the next and the next.

I think it started after one of the young student wives, a friend named Natalie, decided to take her babies home to her parents on weekends. Some of the men made fun of her about "going home to Mother," but I did not think it was amusing at all. In fact, I was bitterly jealous. What bothered me most was that I was a twenty-five-year-old woman, much too old, I rationalized, for a sudden, inexplicable longing for my mother that overshadowed everything else. I wanted to go back to the farm, to find her there, to show off my girls, to share their first steps, to boast about their first teeth. I wanted to be mothered myself, to reverse my role. I could even remember how it felt. The child in me literally ached to be held. Recently a friend who works as a volunteer in a county nursing home told me about an ill, aged woman in her eighties crying out for her "mommy" while she was being bathed. There is no substitute for the mother-child relationship, and I know now the desire never really leaves us, man or woman.

George was patient and helped with the children while I walked and brooded and searched the university and public libraries for books that would help me to understand what on earth was happening to me. But I was lethargic, melancholy, and it was difficult to work because I often stayed awake all night reading. It was the reading that helped me through and opened up a continuing interest in children.

In that searching period in my young womanhood, in those few months before and after our third daughter, Teresa, was born, I read enough about psychology and child development to be convinced that stress starts at birth and in the early years. And I thought about the unmet needs in my own beginning, those childhood experiences, hazy, vague, but tucked away in the nooks and crannies where thoughts and actions are governed. It became clear that the death of my mother was a dominant force in my life and was making me, quite literally, ill.

Dr. Lee Salk says that "suppressing a grief reaction when it is appropriate causes a later manifestation in some physical disturbance that is, in effect, the equivalent of the suppressed grief." According to Lee, at the age of twenty-five I must have had a delayed reaction to a crisis that filled me with desolation, fright, anger, resentment, guilt. The adults in my life, supposedly endowed with unlimited authority and power, had not helped me to cope with these raw feelings or to reverse the tragedy that caused them.

Studies show that bereaved children build up massive defenses if they are not told outright that death is final. They want to know the facts. They want to discern their — and everyone else's — feelings. Conceivably, my own needless suffering might have been avoided. When my kitten died, for instance, I might have been told matter-of-factly that it would not live anymore, or breathe, or eat, or play. The cat might have been buried with dignity in our pet cemetery with the help of an adult imparting the spirit of Donne by telling me that whenever a living things dies it diminishes each of us. When Mother died, I might have been urged to express both my positive and negative memories about her, and to share, share, share my loss. I needed to know the others felt as I did, that they cared as much. My own daughter Ann, when her father-in-law, Sterling "Terry" Mead, died, forthrightly told my three-year-old grandson, Timmy, that his grandfather would not be here anymore, that the doctors could not make him well, but that we all still loved him and would miss him. Timmy eased the finality of death in his own way by saying, "I wish I had two Grandpa Terrys — so one could stay here." We agreed with him. We let him know we all felt the same way, and we left the door open for sharing with him whatever speculation or fantasy made him feel better.

Also, in my own childhood I might have been spared a second dreadful shock that compounded my unwholesome trepidation. I had forgotten about it until that trying period in my pregnancy when I was coming to grips with the notion that trauma in life does not go away, but must be faced. Suddenly another unspeakable ogre, shrouded in the dark recesses of my imagination, was exposed: the belief that I was going to die young. I could remember exactly when I had first learned about it. It was after my mother died and I was in the back seat of the old Plymouth, eavesdropping on an uncharacteristically dramatic conversation between Dad and Grandmother Young. They were talking about a dream an aunt had had. I was captivated until I heard the climax and the description of beautiful Marian, my mother, seated in her heavenly robes in front of a door that opened up and — Eleanor walked in!

Even today I can feel the paralysis that crept from my chest to my fingertips to my toes. I pretended that I wasn't listening. But I felt certain that Dad believed the dream would come true. He seemed resigned about my joining Mother, and I did not doubt that it was going to happen. (Perhaps that is why Dad was so afraid for me to be pregnant and to risk the possibility that I might be in the hospital, alone, and he would not get there in time.)

How cruel the consequences can be when adults speak unthinkingly in front of children! It is too easy to forget that youngsters are people with acute sensitivity. I have a friend who heard her mother jokingly barter her for a piano with a door-to-door salesman. For days thereafter she hid under her bed whenever the doorbell rang. In my own case I took long walks in the alfalfa fields and dramatized my own death until I was spent and grubby and streaked with tears. But as the days passed into months, I learned to hide the secret even from myself. Then I went off to high school and there was so much to do in my new, unfamiliar world that nothing seemed out of place. I was like a piece that fit neatly into the pattern of a jigsaw puzzle, and death was simply no longer a factor.

I wish I had been more insightful in those depressing months that set off Teresa's birth like parentheses. Perhaps then I might have suspected that even though I loved and cared for my pretty, newborn baby, she was somehow being touched by my anxieties during that early symbiotic period in our relationship. I was young and strong and thought I could handle anything, certainly my own emotions. After all, I knew about pregnancy and postpartum blues, and over and over I said to myself, "This too shall pass," which is what happened very soon. My depression left as quickly as it had come. And I did not think about it again until eighteen years later when Teresa herself felt lost and unsure.

Chapter VI

The Circus Years

I WAS ALREADY IN LABOR in the Mitchell Methodist Episcopal Hospital on a sweltering July day in that same
familiar room in which Ann and Susan and Teresa had
been anticipated, when Dr. Harvard Lewis forecast
that our fourth baby would probably be a boy. George
had brought along the newspapers so that between
contractions he could rub my back and we could read
about Adlai Stevenson and the forthcoming 1952 Presidential election. There was no doubt in our minds
that a person with Stevenson's monumental integrity
should lead the country. He was doing exactly what he
had promised to do — talk sense to the American people — and we were excited by his eloquent style.

As we quietly browsed through the newspapers, the
breeze from a little electric fan riffling the pages,

George said suddenly, "Well, if it should be a boy, why don't we name him Steven after Stevenson?" Now, in my mind, July 27, 1952, the birthday of our son, Steve, symbolically marks George's beginning in politics.

In reality, Stevenson's defeat, the overwhelming renunciation of his ideas by South Dakotans, merely hastened George's move from the classroom into the world of more pragmatic ideas. It was not an easy step, and for several months we weighed our new-begotten financial security and George's promising future as a teacher against an offer by Ward Clark, the South Dakota Democratic chairman, to organize the state's almost nonexistent party. The political option appeared ludicrous to everybody but us. But as a historian George believed that good government required a two-party system, and South Dakota was barreling the other way; and as an ambitious young man with a sensitive social conscience and a wide range of interests, he felt compelled, as he says now, "to move onto a larger platform." So, in early 1953, absolutely contrary to the advice of every friend he consulted, he resigned as head of the history department of Dakota Wesleyan University to become the executive secretary of what was left of the state party — a job nobody else wanted. He told me at the time that he had to trust his instincts.

Our lives were turning outward again, and I liked that. Yet it was not pleasant for me to realize that George was going to be away, doing everything himself to build up a grassroots political organiza-

tion — speaking, putting out press releases, driving
hour after hour across country roads in search of Democrats who would contribute funds to the party and,
more specifically, to his own salary, for which he was
responsible. Now it was two, sometimes three months
without pay; a bank loan; then the cycle over and over.
Gone was the relative freedom of academic life which
had made it possible for him, out of plain old-
fashioned consideration for me, to help wash dishes,
scrub floors, vacuum, change diapers, and comfort
four little children. Instead, he was up and on the
road at dawn, often for a week at a time. Moreover, as
a family, we had lost a certain measure of privacy because George had had the effrontery to challenge the
entrenched Republican politicians — he called them
"the closed corporation, the same little gang." But
when he came back to our little house in Mitchell, it
seemed worth it. He was like a different person when
he described the colorful, authentic human beings with
whom he was getting acquainted, the South Dakotans
who saw politics in terms of day-to-day life. They were
free spirits and they pleased him. "It's easy to explain
why I am a Democrat," one old individualist explained.
"When Republicans are in power, the interest rates go
up. When Democrats are in power, hog prices go up."
(George still recalls the incongruity of discovering a
grizzled, gravy-stained Democrat in an isolated shack
in the northwest part of the state, who was a fascinating world traveler with valuable political insights and
electric ideas.) When he first wrote to the sixty-seven

county chairmen, telling them about his new job, only
six replied, not including one who owned a general
store and would talk politics only in the back room
because, he said, "I'd be out of business if my cus-
tomers knew." But within two years, even though it
was still risky for voters to admit Democratic affiliation
publicly, George had compiled on three-by-five cards
the names of thirty-five thousand Democrats, or at
least people who would give him half a chance to explain his views.

In 1955 our last child, Mary Kay, was born, and
George announced he was running for the U.S. House
of Representatives. He had decided that, although
Congressman Harold Lovre was a popular, three-term
incumbent, it might be possible to defeat him with a
vigorous person-to-person campaign. Friends were
less sanguine about his chances, but George is never
swayed much by advice and still follows his own instincts; in fact, we both believe that real friends are
often overly cautious because they do not want you to
be hurt or to appear ridiculous.

George recently described the plunge into that first
campaign this way: "We had five children and no income at all the minute I announced for Congress. My
wife did all the work at home. Some people gave me
political contributions and some gave me money to
support my family — which I did on $4000. I spent
$13,000 on the campaign and ended up $3000 in debt.
I drove our car until it literally collapsed at 130,000

miles. George Cunningham, who is still with me, volunteered his time and for a brief period I had a volunteer woman secretary, Pat Buchanan. They were my
entire staff. It was very hard at first. I'd shake people's hands and say, 'I'm George McGovern,' and I'd
give them a little card identifying me with a quick
sketch of my program. Some people would just tear
them in two and drop the pieces at my feet."

In retrospect, our poverty seems more humorous
than it was at the time. He and George Cunningham
had to sell big, saucer-sized campaign buttons to pay
for expenses — even for gas for the car. And sometimes supporters gave them food instead of money,
which was all right with me because it meant a richer
casserole or meat sauce with the spaghetti. But it was
almost a knockout blow when they did not recover a
twenty-dollar bill that had fallen through a hole in
George's pocket at a picnic — he went back at night to
search the picnic grounds, prowling around on all
fours with a flashlight.

I helped at campaign headquarters whenever I
could, but it was impossible to feel effective with five
children at home, ranging in age from one to eleven
years. And it had been a cruel summer. In June Phyllis' young husband, Robert Peterson, had died, leaving
her shattered, with two little babies. And in August
Dad had had a heart attack. I was not there and
learned later that he had died within minutes. That
hot afternoon George and I had taken Ann and Sue
and Teresa to a television station in Sioux Falls for the

first time. They had wanted to see how their father "got in the picture," and we thought an afternoon together would help a bit to make up for the increasing confusion of their family life. I was having such a good time that I paid no attention to the telephone call George received as we arrived at the station. Later, when we were driving home, he quietly told me that Dad was gone.

After his death I remembered Dad not for the hard times but the happy ones, such as the summer he came to Colorado to be with George and me and Ann, Sue, Teresa, and Ila and her little Sharon. The girls were all under five, and Dad and I watched them while George researched the Ludlow Massacre for his dissertation. Dad was a good grandfather. How he laughed as we drove over the Great Divide, so high that we were literally on top of the clouds, and the children kept chirping, "God? Jesus? Where are you? Where are you?"

When I am asked if I have always campaigned for George, I usually say "yes" even though I did practically nothing that could be deemed political in that first race in 1956. Chiefly I tried to be stoic because George was being criticized harshly for being a "radical," a "red," even a "communist," because he had advocated recognition of China and her entrance into the United Nations. Such contemptuousness was new to me. Once I unexpectedly lashed out with a few public words against smear tactics at a sedate tea for women; another time I burst into tears on the street when a friend offered sympathetic words; and I was moved enough to cry when a fine but inarticulate supporter walked into headquarters and pulled out a five-dollar bill, saying, "I feel terrible about what is going on. I don't know what to do, but maybe this will help." Finally I even stopped reading the newspapers. But on the crisp Monday before election George and I were suddenly convinced that we were going to win. That is about all I remember until we started packing the kids and our shabby old furniture into a Ford station wagon and headed for the nation's capital.

I call our first decade in politics "the circus years." It was a risky, vagrant, promising period of simultaneous juggling acts in three separate rings. In one ring was our obligation to the small band of flinty South Dakotans who had doggedly helped to elect George to the House. In another ring was our obligation to understand Washington's fragmented legislative machinery, its elusive power center, its beehive social structure. And in the third ring, a kaleidoscopic center ring for me, there was our obligation to each other and to the family.

On the icy January morning George was sworn into Congress, we all dressed up and drove to the Hill. I managed to observe most of the ceremony only because Fish Bait Miller, the Doorkeeper of the House, offered to baby-sit in his office with Mary Kay, a bubbling, noisy toddler, and little Steve got bored quickly and fell asleep in my lap in the family gallery, where I

had lined up the older little girls. I longed for
Dad. If he had lived to see George take the oath as a
member of Congress, it would have been a highlight in
his life. And he would have been thrilled that George
introduced an agricultural bill on his first day, and in
the following months secured the passage of more leg-
islation than any of the forty-four newly elected colleagues who had been sworn in with him.

On New Year's Eve day we moved into a nice, four-
bedroom house — no down payment and three
mortgages — in suburban Chevy Chase, next door to
Hubert and Muriel Humphrey. They had children
the ages of some of ours, extra beds, pots of coffee,
good advice, and shared a similar Midwest heritage,
which meant a lot to both of us. We were especially
grateful when they suggested that we all go together to
Eisenhower's second inaugural ball, our first formal
function as a part of official Washington. George
came home with rented tails and I put on a long, iridescent taffeta dress I had brought from home. (Actually I had bought two before I left because each had
been marked down to $3.97.) Next door at the
Humphreys' we posed for a photographer with Hubert
and Muriel and Minnesota's Governor Orville Freeman
and his wife, Jane. Then we were chauffeured to the
ball in the long, black limousine assigned to them. I
was wide-eyed at the scene I had imagined many times:
the impressive statesmen looking down at us from
boxes ringing the dance floor, the sophisticated women
of the diplomatic corps, the elegant couples dancing.

There is a subtle sense of togetherness at an inaugural ball, a pervasive feeling that each person there is more than an observer at a pageant, rather a thread in an enduring tapestry. In fact, I was so excited about being there that I was not the least disillusioned to realize that I could have worn a burlap bag and not been noticed and that governors are accorded royal treatment while freshmen Congressmen rate very, very low on the protocol totem pole.

Without much thought I plunged into activities expected of political wives in Washington — clubs, lectures, tours, luncheons, teas; many nights, after preparing dinner and helping with schoolwork, I would find a baby sitter, hop into a cab, and meet George downtown at a reception or dinner party. At first we accepted every invitation we received because we thought we had to. Then we realized we could pick and choose. Later I remembered those days when I read the journal of Ellen Maury Slayden, the wife of a Texas Congressman in Washington from 1897 until 1919, and a woman with whom I felt rapport — she was under five feet tall, married to a Democratic peace candidate, hated clubs, read a lot, and kept voluminous notebooks. "It is a distinct advantage to have known Washington before," she wrote in 1897. "An invitation came from a 'Baroness' something, and instinct prompted me not even to send a card of acknowledgment. I have heard since that she took the title from the given name of a departed husband who made a fortune keeping a bar, and that new

Congressmen's wives are her favorite prey. Some Texas girls told me that I 'missed a lovely time' at the tea; that the Baroness was 'real elegant' and 'was coming to call' — just as I feared."

At the Congressional Club Mrs. Clifford Davis, wife of the Congressman from Tennessee, told those of us who were new in Washington that if we did what we were supposed to do we would call immediately on at least four hundred government officials — which nobody had done since Mrs. Clark Thompson of Texas hired a cab and left her calling cards all over town. Protocol was the code of "international courtesy," she explained, and "no more than a simple set of rules mixed with courtesy and common sense." Then she admitted with good humor that the way things were done in Washington was exactly opposite from the way things were done back home: in the capital, for instance, a husband precedes his wife in a receiving line; a newcomer makes the first call and *never* expects to see the person she is calling on; and the ranking guest leaves first instead of last, and *always* by eleven o'clock. Then there were bewildering instructions about addressing officials, and I learned that I could say "Mr. President" or "Mr. Ambassador," but that I should say "Senator Brown" and, preferably, "Congressman Smith"; and that in seating guests a wife outranks her husband, women in Congress outrank wives, but Senate wives outrank women Representatives; and that, no matter what the custom is in Woonsocket or Rapid City, I should either take both gloves off or leave both on when going down a receiving line, *never* half and half. I remember fondly that Carrie Davis ended her little speech on protocol by saying, "Don't do as I do — but do as I say!" That was always a source of comfort when I felt guilt-stricken about not leaving my card, carefully dog-earred in the upper right-hand corner as instructed by Carrie, at the doors of members of Congress who were senior to George. In fact, I did not go calling at all.

Although we did many things we did not want to do, there were the memorable times: meeting Eleanor Roosevelt, Indira Gandhi, Harold Wilson, John and Robert Kennedy, and catching a first glimpse of Senators Joe McCarthy, Everett Dirksen, Stuart Symington, and many other Washington celebrities. And Adlai Stevenson — I told him about his namesake, Steve, and added that Teresa had once asked if God, Jesus, and Adlai were the same person. "I'm afraid that version of the Trinity would be hard to sell," he answered. I wrote home about the special occasions. My family and friends in South Dakota liked the details of the more glamorous side of the nation's capital. When I met Queen Elizabeth, our Grandma Ethel Owen, not a relative but a beloved South Dakota friend who helped me with the children, wrote a little poem about how I had practiced curtseying and had made a blue velveteen dress with a hat to match in honor of the queen of England.

Until I had the chance to travel across the country, I had forgotten that people tend to think everyday life in

Washington is somehow uncommon, constantly vibrant. Even now I am asked, "What? *You* in a railroad station? I thought you would travel by private jet," or "I can't believe it! A Senator's wife putting her own groceries in the car!" I feel tempted to point out that I feel lucky when I have a car, that when we first moved to Washington I drove only one day a week in a frantic attempt to carry out the logistics for a household of seven. On that day George usually rode to work with Hubert. Many times I ached for Woonsocket and Mitchell, for cottonwoods and elms, for schools, shops, markets, doctors' offices, more often than not sprinkled with dear friends or relatives, all within walking distance. Often, very often, we longed for more casual living. I think that is why George and Hubert loved to gather up the neighborhood gang on Saturdays and buy ice-cream cones at Giffords' and then come home and lounge around the back yard in the sun.

George was restless and worked hard. Right after he was sworn into Congress he started serving his home-state constituents by laying down a law that every letter from South Dakota had to be answered within twenty-four hours. He had no intention of being a one-term politician, and started planning quickly for the 1958 campaign. Once more, friends advised him against running, particularly against his opponent, Joe Foss, a Marine Corps flying ace who had been governor for two terms. Joe was not only a popular governor, but a national, heavily publicized celebrity. Moreover, he was backed by the state's powerful Republican

Senator, Karl Mundt, who was beginning to sense that George might one day covet his seat in the U.S. Senate.

George described that election to a reporter this way: "Joe's campaign didn't go too well, especially a debate we had on TV and radio. On election eve Joe copied a thing I'd done, a little five-minute appearance with my family. So the picture comes on TV and Joe is at the governor's mansion — the show is live — and he has all his kids around him and his wife and his dog. He had part of his talk on the Teleprompter, and as he started reading, one of his kids started reading it too, but about one word behind him. Then Joe's effort to make the kid stop got the dog frightened and excited. When Joe reached down to pat the dog, it growled at him. Then the governor in desperation turned to his wife and said, 'Honey, is there anything you want to say?' She said, 'About what?' He said, 'Well, about the campaign.' She said, 'I guess not.' I was elected easily."

George and I still feel great empathy for that family, trying so hard to help, feeling inadequate. Politics does not come easily to everybody. Our own children, we know now, were more personally touched by early campaigns than we thought: little Susan, hurt and astonished, passionately muttering, "I can't *stand* it!" as she switched off a TV program critical of her dad; Teresa, gregarious, competitive, who bought candy bars for a nickel and sold them for nine cents to swell our Congressional campaign chest, telling a toy-store owner, "You could do much better if you put my dad's poster in your window" (the chairman of the Young Republicans announced later that "maybe we could have beaten George McGovern, but we could not beat George McGovern — and his Terry"); young Steve, a sweaty little hand in mine, holding back as we entered a Republican-owned store for Cub Scout equipment, saying, "Aren't you *afraid* to go in?"; and the same young boy, during a winter in Washington, asking, "Mommy, when are we going to move back into the house in Mitchell where Daddy used to play with me?"

George says he could not have pursued a career in politics if I had been fighting him about being away from the children; I knew he would have given it up if I had ever told him it was too difficult for his family. In 1972 he told a reporter, "I can see points at which I would have gone out of public life. It's all been so uphill all along. Eleanor's opposition would have been just too much opposition. Those long days away, particularly when the youngsters were little and really needed me — that is a source of sadness. I've had times when I wondered if it wasn't too big a price to pay." Yet in retrospect Steve, for example, recollects mostly the good times together. After he was grown, he wrote this: "I remember when used to travel from South Dakota to Washington in the car, the whole family, with everyone relaxed and my father telling terrible jokes and telling us about the places we were passing. To my young mind, he was the wisest, best man in the world. I felt so secure and happy about life. How could I fail with such a father?"

I always knew I could count on George if I needed him. He was more patient and effective with the children than I was when he intervened in squabbles or gave one of the youngsters his undivided attention or offered sound and sensible solutions to childish woes. They were mother-deaf to me. Yet I always enjoyed being a mother. If I had another chance, I would spend more time with my family, particularly that valuable "lap time" when babies learn to trust and emulate other human beings. I would not let the housework dominate me; rather, I would enjoy my babies, enjoy those moments as they first shadowboxed to find their little hands, made sweet gurgling sounds, said words, turned over, poked, tasted, sniffed, crawled, walked, talked; I would watch with greater interest those tentative signals of independence, the pragmatic application of concepts, the literal interpretation of events. And I would be much more aware of my own influence on impressionable small children. I would try to remember that I was playing a part in those magic years. How well I remember the tender way my mother sang to Ila and me! When Sue was a young woman, she brought back to me from Ireland a musical stein because it played a little tune I had crooned to her when she was little. It was meaningful to her. Since then I have tried to rock and sing to my grandchildren.

When I was a young mother, I learned much about myself through my children and from wiser adults less emotionally involved in dealing with the normal daily

stages of their development. When it was time for
Mary Kay to go to kindergarten, for instance, she was
so distraught that for the first week I stayed in class
and sat close enough so that she could touch me. I
know now that she was insecure because she sensed
that I did not want her to leave home. She was the
youngest, the last child to play beneath my feet, and
even though I was looking forward to a few hours of
freedom, it was the end of an era for me. Without her
teacher, Mrs. Fletcher, I do not think I could have
turned my back and walked away. But when I did,
Mary Kay's crucially important confidence in herself
came fast. I was again forced to remember that one
can never cling to the past. And the first time Steve
climbed a tree and crawled out on a limb, I thought he
was much too young, too unskilled, to be up there by
himself, and I demanded that he come down. But
George contradicted me and called, "Say, Steve, how
does the world look from up there? Tell us about it."
The little boy enjoyed a moment of self-sufficiency,
then climbed down again. George had offered him
the courage to face needless fear, as he himself had
done during World War II, while I had offered Steve
the feeling that he should be afraid.

I did resent endless housework — I always have —
and had many surges of self-pity. Once when I was
scrubbing the kitchen floor, I threw a rag across the
mud-tracked linoleum and decided I was going to get
out of the house and *do* something. I remember wish-
ing I could be like W. R. Ronald, the editor of the

Mitchell *Daily Republic,* a public-spirited man with great capability. Dad had always read his editorials, usually aloud, and I had admired him since I was a little girl. But I was not a W. R. Ronald; I was the young wife of a responsible public servant, and a woman who could help five children grow into whole adults, which up until that time I had considered a simple, indisputable fact, and not a long, often difficult uncertainty. Even though the housework was routine, monotonous, mechanical, dull, and certainly not stimulating, I told myself I would not turn off my mind. Washington was a fascinating place, and I was fortunate to be on the fringes of power; even if it meant scouring pots and pans one minute, it sometimes meant chatting with the nation's most erudite public men and women the next. During that period I made naive but firm resolutions to scrub floors only once a week, no matter how crusty they were, to change more often the list of vocabulary words I kept pinned over the sink, and to spend more time delving into books about psychology, sociology, and other fields. I was determined to help with George's career, not only by taking responsibility for the family, but by contributing ideas. In fact, I never considered it "George's" career — it was "ours."

I thought a lot about us, that center ring, in those circus days. Most often any times of contemplation came as I drove the station wagon, stuffed with fidgety children, year after year, hour after hour, between Washington and South Dakota, pushing the car down the highway as far as I could go at a stretch before everything fell apart in the back seat, sometimes feeling pretty resentful because George would be flying overhead in the opposite direction to keep some important commitment. But I knew I was fortunate to be in accord with his political goals. We were starry-eyed and zealous about our country. Our aims could sustain us. And at least for a few years as a political wife — just about eight years, to be exact — I was able to convince myself easily, even when overcome with weariness from coping with our absolutely chaotic household, or with loneliness for George, or with apprehension about being the faultless mother my own mother had been, that I was in the right place at the right time doing the right thing.

By 1960, when George decided his chances were good to beat the incumbent South Dakota Senator Karl Mundt, I urged him to try. I had no qualms about risking our security this time. Anything was better than campaigning for re-election every two years, living with one foot in South Dakota and the other in Washington with a preoccupied husband and five growing children who had no idea where they belonged. This time it was an ideological race against a man who held opposite points of view on practically every issue. But he was a popular incumbent in a predominantly Republican state, and even though the polls initially were strong in our favor, the campaign soon sagged badly. That year the Catholicism of the Democratic Presidential candidate, John F. Kennedy, was a big issue at home. I remember finding out early that it was a mistake for me to deliver campaign literature to people who lived next door to churches — that was about all that I had time to do on George's behalf — because invariably they included a few Protestant church people with blazing anti-Catholic prejudice. One woman even told me that Catholicism was unconstitutional. Both Jack and Bob Kennedy came out to South Dakota; after a speech Jack gave at the Corn Palace, it is reported that he later said to his brother, "Bobby, I think we just cost that man a seat in the Senate." And in the last down days, just before George was defeated, we asked for help and Bob left his brother's campaign and flew out to Watertown for a rally. We never forgot that.

The 1960 defeat was especially hard for George because he felt negative about his opponent and positive about his own worth in government. Ann, who was fifteen at the time, recalls how crushed we were, but says that her memories are strong that George handled winning and losing in more or less the same way, as far as the children were concerned. "That night he took us aside and said that what had happened was not going to shatter our family, or damage it, or change it in any way," she recalls. "It was reassuring." A few days later President-elect Kennedy called from Palm Beach. We were having dinner with friends when the call came through, and I could hear George on the telephone, saying, "No, Jack, it wasn't your fault I lost. I did that all by myself." When he came back to the table, he was grinning and reported, "He said not to make any plans until he talks to me again."

George believes that both his defeat in 1960 and the denial of a cabinet post in the Kennedy administration — he wanted to be Secretary of Argriculture — were fortuitous. Instead, President Kennedy appointed him to be director of "Food for Peace," a program later judged by Arthur Schlesinger to be "the greatest unseen weapon of Kennedy's Third World policy," and by George as "a glamorous, humanitarian effort." In less romantic terms the program was the Agricultural Trade Development and Assistance Act, or Public Law 480, designed to help the needy overseas and to unburden the United States of some of our vast surplus commodities. In those days, difficult as it may be to realize now, it was cheaper to give away America's food than to store it. Among other things "Food for Peace" provided a school-lunch program in Peru that caused school attendance to swell by forty per cent; and nutritious calories for starving *niños* in Central America; and relief for millions of hungry babies, dying from ordinary childhood diseases because their bodies were too weak to resist. George told me that he had gone into one little dwelling in Recife, Brazil, and had seen a ravaged young woman holding her dying child closely. His interpreter explained that the child was dying from a simple case of the measles, complicated by malnutrition, just as another child in the family had died the previous day.

But "Food for Peace" was also a monumental headache for George to administer, a gigantic problem, wrapped in so much bureaucratic red tape that it was difficult to accomplish the mission — to get food, grain, dry milk, and other foodstuffs to the impoverished nations of the world. "Oh, Eleanor," he said to me one night in frustration, "you would not believe it. There are twenty people in the U.S. Government waiting to stop progress for every one person with a new idea." Trying to do something about the world food problem was a unique lesson for him in working within the system from a different vantage point.

Whenever I think of those days, I remember Mary McGrory's description of Washington during the administration of Jack Kennedy: "When he came to the White House, suddenly everyone saw what the New Frontier was going to mean. It meant a poet at the Inauguration; it meant swooping around Washington, dropping in on delighted and flustered old friends; it meant going to the airport in zero weather without an overcoat; it meant a rocking chair and having the Hickory Hill seminar at the White House when Bobby and Ethel were out of town; it meant fun at presidential press conferences. It meant dash, glamour, glitter, charm. It meant a new era of enlightenment and verve; it meant Nobel Prize winners dancing in the lobby; it meant authors and actors and poets and Shakespeare in the East Room."

For many of us those stirring recollections are veiled by darker memories. I don't think I will ever be able to separate the joy from the sorrow. The night John Kennedy's body lay in the Bethesda Naval Hospital, our whole family pressed into the car and drove aimlessly around the woods nearby. That was all we could do for him or for ourselves. George and I still remember: standing in a drizzle at a plowing contest near Sioux Falls to hear him speak; riding on the Presidential airplane, the "Caroline"; the telephone call from Palm Beach; dining at the White House and feeling a part of its history. The night before President Kennedy's funeral, after the family had gone to bed, I sat alone and watched TV at the kitchen table, listening to the beautiful music, drinking in the glorious scenes of America. I could not reach the hurt, and I have never cried before or since as I did then. George and I went to the rotunda services; at 2:00 A.M. the children and I and a friend of one of the girls, Charles Drew, impulsively drove back up to the Hill; and the next day we all went downtown and saw the world leaders precede John F. Kennedy's cortege. Some of our family finally went back to the car to get warm, but Sue and I, chilled to the bone, stood on the curb for a very long time.

Perhaps the happier, more glittering times are dim because I was in and out of Washington for weeks at a time during Jack Kennedy's administration. In spite of my exhilaration about George's role in the new government, I had my own strong convictions that the children and I should stay in South Dakota, in one place, at least long enough for them to have one full term in the same school. As George has said often, everything at home has a place, a specific definition; it is easier to find one's self. We were both raised with a small-town sense of community — a need for family, neighbors, church, schools. They had provided for us a foundation and a sense of personal security. I thought that the children deserved such beginnings, or perhaps I needed home myself as I faced up to the fact that George would be traveling even more as "Food for Peace" director than he had as a Congressman.

But I was as guilty about living away from George as I had been about constantly uprooting the family. So I was glad when school was over and we packed up the car and headed back across the highways to Washington. I found George in bed. He had been infected by a contaminated needle used for an inoculation in preparation for a mission President Kennedy had asked him to undertake in Brazil. He was in the early stages of hepatitis, pale, severely ill, too weak to feed himself. Within a couple of weeks I realized that he was already planning to spend his long convalescence mapping out another race for the United States Senate.

In 1962 for the first time I campaigned actively for George. We could not bear the thought of another defeat, especially since his opponent, the very conservative Joe Bottum, centered his campaign on the contentions that George was both a flaming radical and a "pawn of the Kennedys." George, on the other hand, was giving speeches to the farmer, saying, "I have seen in all parts of the globe wheat and milk and corn from

South Dakota clearing up the swamplands of hunger on which communism breeds. This nation has no stronger asset in our competition with Mr. Khrushchev than the American farmer."

It was stimulating to campaign with George. I had never felt more than a spectator on the public scene, and I enjoyed taking the initiative in meeting new people, though I was embarrassed by the brief, superficial conversations that were necessary because we were inevitably overscheduled. And my size — I am barely five feet tall — was a handicap. It had always been a problem trying to walk with George easily; but it was worse to be caught in crowds pressing around him, a six-footer, when I was submerged in a sea of elbows and surfaced only when we were seated on platforms, where my feet sometimes did not touch the floor. Standing in receiving lines, handling what we now call "mix and mingle" events — those traditional women's brunches, luncheons, coffees, teas — was a little easier; my memory, which I always fear will fail me, served better than I expected. And I quickly learned to feel easy with strangers by offering a hearty, firm handshake and by saying, "Hello, I would like to meet you," then adding, "I am Mrs. George McGovern," rather than the other way around. The thought of publicly addressing myself to issues was unthinkable to me then. Besides, nobody asked me!

It was on October 4, just a month away from a victory we were already beginning to savor, when the campaign came to a crashing halt. George suddenly felt faint and feverish, and everything indicated that he had hepatitis again. He needed time for medical tests before he talked to the press. He needed time to think things through. But even more immediately he needed someone to take his place at a rally the next day in Sisseton, about 190 miles away from Mitchell.

I knew I could do it, even if the only way to get there was for me to drive across the prairie nonstop. So I gathered up Steve, then ten years old, to be my navigator, handed him a map, and told him to find Highway 81 and keep me on course. Once when I grew drowsy and pulled over in a ditch off the highway, he sat quietly while I slept for half an hour, then wakened me exactly on time as he had promised to do. Only then did it dawn on me that I would have to speak to the crowd expecting George, and the thought filled me with such anxiety that, when Steve excitedly pointed out that Highway 81 ended up in Canada, I seriously considered going all the way.

I do not have the vaguest recollection of what I said or did that evening. The high point was spotting constituents asking for Steve's autograph. But after that, after we knew that George was too ill to travel but could lie in his bed and write press releases and manage the campaign, I drove all over the state with a bottle of milk on the front seat of the car, got up before crowds and said a few words of greeting — always leaving the heavy stuff to good Democratic friends — and concluded with, "You will be *hearing* from George, but you will not be *seeing* him." By November 7 I myself was almost disabled by having been politician, wife, nurse, mother, but my self-confidence was soaring; this really was "our" campaign, not just George's. And when we won the election, that sweet victory, I felt that I had earned my place as the wife of a Senator by proving to myself that I could rise to any occasion if I had to. We still called it "our victory," but for me there was a special secret triumph involved.

Chapter VII

Family Bonds

W<small>HEN WE SETTLED BACK</small> in Washington in late 1962, I decided that it was time to take inventory, time to add to depleted resources before going forward, time to have time for me. I was weary, physically and emotionally. I felt I deserved an interlude to be self-indulgent, to touch base with myself.

Quietly but methodically I dropped out of clubs and forums and declined invitations to the big political receptions I had perfunctorily attended as a Congressman's wife. With equal precision I started considering my own hungers, attacking books I had piled up for years, satiating myself, hit or miss, with volumes of ideas about everything that caught my fancy — children, archeology, politics, literature, philosophy, and religion. At least daily I thumbed through Harry

Emerson Fosdick's printed sermons, *The Meaning of Faith, The Meaning of Prayer, The Meaning of Service,* or *On Being Fit To Live With.* The last-named book, the only Fosdick volume I still have left intact, is so dear to me that I keep it in our safe, carefully mended with Scotch tape.

I read mostly on our glassed-in back porch, getting up only to replenish raisins by the door for the birds, or to drop grain in my bird feeders, or to study a chickadee, a titmouse, a cardinal, or my favorites, the mockingbirds. It was enchanting to discover birds again, and I bought illustrated books so that I could identify new ones, and played records so that I could compare, say, the song of the meadowlark in Maryland with the song of the meadowlark in the fields near Woonsocket. When the feeders were empty, the mockingbirds scolded me through the glass; and in mating season the brilliant male cardinals from the arch of the trellis picked sunflower seeds out of my hand and fed their mates.

Now, with the children older and the backyard empty of toys, I could raise roses. At night my arms ached from lugging around sacks of peat, sand, fertilizer, and digging and weeding and watering, planting and replanting, most often following the advice of my next-door neighbor, Muriel Humphrey, who is one of the best dirt gardeners I have ever known. More than once I was so engrossed in my garden that I was oblivious of rain until I was drenched and muddy.

Books, birds, flowers, solitude — simple and improbable; much, much more than nostalgia for my child-hood; an almost physical need for nourishment from nature, for sustenance from the earth and sky. For a brief period — all too brief — every morning when I awoke I said to myself, "This wonderful day is all mine!"

For the second time George and I took stock of our-selves and our marriage. We were not the same peo-ple who had married in 1943 and were symbolically re-newed after World War II. We found our bonds were strong. Over a decade had passed, during which both of us traveled separate paths toward the same destina-tion, and it seemed almost as though our mutual inter-est in power — that little bit of power that can bring about a little bit of change — was what had carried our marriage along. Perhaps today our marriage would be described as more "open" than those of most of our contemporaries; certainly "togetherness" was not a prerequisite for what we shared with each other. It was true that sometimes political life stretched out the physical and emotional distance between us; yet our ties were more compelling than uninterrupted per-sonal felicity. Politics and family were everything, and we were unabashedly idealistic about both. We had been raised to believe that responsibility and commit-ment to others, as well as to ourselves, was the only way to live or to grow, and that personal growth was the ev-idence of living. Within politics and family, we thought, there was unlimited opportunity.

And there were things to be done: in the world, ra-

tional analysis of America's growing involvement in a
dangerous little war in a place called Vietnam; and in
the family, coping with five demanding adolescents
who were beginning to rock my complacency.

Neither one of us guessed what we were in for.

In spite of the current debate about the coming ob-
solescence of the American family and those dramatic
observations that the nuclear family has become the
cradle of evil and that test-tube babies will replace
childbirth, I think that the institution called family is
the center of strength in society. I know that the family, as we have known it, cannot remain forever the
same, nor should it. Its structure must change. But I
want it to survive. My own family has been to me like
a small community within which I have been able to
embrace from day to day the whole human experience — sometimes stifling, ofttimes broadening; many
times providing love, security, concern; other times
provoking rivalry, guilt, anger. I look back now and
know that the most valuable insights gained in my life
did not rise like genies from a bottle, or pop up out of
pages in a book, but were thrust upon me when I
coped with the myriad interrelationships in my own
family.

The adolescent years of my children were unlike
anything I had experienced and I had no model for
my role. I told my family early that I wanted them to
tell me when I was unfair. But it hurt me when they
did. I wanted to provide them with the tools to become independent. I wanted to keep them close too.

The family farm on the plains outside Woonsocket, South Dakota, where Eleanor McGovern grew up.

Eleanor's parents — Marion Payne Stegeberg (who died when Eleanor was eleven) and Earl Stegeberg.

Eleanor (left) and her twin sister, Ila, in 1922.

Eleanor (right) and Ila at the age of seven, with their mother and little sister Phyllis.

Eleanor (right) and Ila at their high school graduation in Woonsocket, 1939.

Pinning on Lieutenant George McGovern's wings at Flight Cadet School graduation in Pampa, Texas, 1943 — shortly after their marriage.

George and Eleanor McGovern, reunited after the war years.

The McGovern family in Mitchell, South Dakota, in the mid-1950's. Clockwise from left: Susan, Teresa, Ann (their oldest child), George, Mary Kay (the youngest), Eleanor, and Steven.

On George's first Congressional campaign in 1956. The children from left: Ann, Teresa, Susan, and Steven.

Freshman Congressman and Mrs. George S. McGovern, photographed at Senator and Mrs. Hubert Humphrey's house before attending President Eisenhower's second Inaugural Ball, January 20, 1957. Eleanor is wearing the "long, iridescent dress I had brought from home — actually I had bought two before I left because each had been marked down to $3.97."

At the Democratic National Convention in Chicago,
August, 1968.

Top: The wives of the three major candidates —
Abigail McCarthy, Muriel Humphrey, Eleanor
McGovern.

Bottom: With her family before her first press conference at the Blackstone Hotel ballroom. Front row,
from left: Mrs. Ann Mead, Mrs. Susan Rowen, Eleanor,
and Teresa. Back row: Wilbur Mead, Jim Rowen,
Steven, and Mary Kay.

With Steve, watching the end of the 1968 Convention
on TV in the McGovern suite at the Blackstone Hotel.

At home in Washington before the 1972 Democratic
National Convention. From left: Mary Kay, Timmy
Mead, Teresa, Ann Mead with Kevin, Susan Rowan
with Matthew, Eleanor, George, and Steven.

Bottom and opposite:
At Miami Beach during the 1972 Convention:

Eleanor and Ila (right)

Top: In the McGoverns' Doral Hotel Suite, George holds his grandson Matthew.

Middle: Eleanor and Teresa.

Bottom: Eleanor happily waving to the crowds from the family box in Convention Hall just after George had won the nomination on the night of July 12. Standing behind her from left: Teresa, Ann Mead, Steven, Henry Kimelman (the campaign financial director), David Harris (Secret Service), and Mary Hoyt.

Working and learning during the Presidential campaign.

Top: On a "listening tour" in a Baltimore dress factory, Eleanor takes shorthand notes in one of her black notebooks.

Bottom: Visiting the Children's Center in Oakland, California, a privately funded, 24-hour day care center.

On a motorcade in Ohio on Labor Day, 1972. Walking on
left is Secret Service Agent Skip Williams, assigned to
Eleanor McGovern throughout the campaign.

Aboard the "Dakota Queen II," George's campaign plane,
flying back to Washington on November 8, 1972, the day
after the election defeat — Eleanor standing behind
Margot Hahn (left) and Mary Hoyt.

At home in South Dakota — the Black Hills.

I was eager for them to sacrifice for George; after all, I pointed out, he was not only trying to provide food, shelter, and clothing for them, but a better future. Even at the time I knew my expectations were unreasonable and I steeled myself against failure as I doled out appropriate measures of discipline and trust to five singular young persons.

Ann: tempestuous, highly visible; flame-cheeked like my mother; sometimes revealing her innermost thoughts in little notes carefully exposed where I could find them; in 1972 candidly confessing to a national magazine writer that growing up for her had been hard because, even though there had been "very special, precious times" with her father, he had been immersed in Congressional activities and had kept "physically slipping away."

Susan: porcelain strength; a feminine version of George; the passion of her personality seldom revealed except through the windows of her eyes — a tear over beautiful music, a burning glance; overcompensating for shyness by being a good student, a good girl, a daughter who placed miniature arrangements of fresh flowers around the house and put herself to bed if she felt sick.

Teresa: compatible, open; we called her our "ray of sunshine"; an appealing clown who imitated her father by giving silly nicknames to the rest of us; a girl always striking chords of cheer in others; the middle child, that uninteresting position in the family — who lost and then found herself.

Steve: all McGovern; bright, holding his talent in

close rein; an independent only brother, who rolled down hills instead of walking, climbed over fences instead of opening gates, and once wore a fringed buckskin jacket like a second skin, summer and winter, until the cuffs were up to his elbows.

Mary Kay: the adored baby; a stylish, stormy teenager with queenly carriage; an original with an original vocabulary; all rhythm, even when she clacked away at night typing poems, novels, and letters to her many friends.

All of my children tell me that I overreacted to their teen-age problems. I think most parents do. When children are small, mothers, particularly, give more than they get. But in the adolescent years it feels the other way around, at least. Suddenly there is not much time left. You want your children to be better than you are; but you are self-critical, uncertain, and almost absurdly handicapped by feelings of inadequacy. Russell Baker once wrote about parenthood in terms of the "evening guilt wallow" that he shared with his wife, during which they came to blame themselves for the war, campus disorder, white racism, and dental caries — all of which their children blamed them for. Doing their best did not seem enough. It was a bit like that at our house.

I worried about defiance, audacity, recklessness, those missing ingredients in my own teen-age years. Why on earth would Ann skip school? What was Susan thinking about when she played the piano at full crescendo so that I could not hear her sister back the car out of the garage? How could those two older girls be so harsh to me and to each other, so ferociously competitive, yet such a formidable team? I am not sure if I was overly permissive or too authoritarian in those days. Undoubtedly a bit of both. Not long ago Ann recalled that she was never really punished, nor did George and I lay down a lot of expectations — "just general kinds of themes." She remembers that I was generally "sympathetic" and kissed everybody good night and stuck to my guns about each person carrying part of the load of the housework. And she remembers that her father once demanded that one of Sue's boy friends leave the house because he had stayed long past curfew time, then the next day brought home for her a little charm because he knew she had been humiliated in front of her date. "Dad made us feel like we were persons, not children," Ann says approvingly. And Sue said to me last year, "You and Dad drummed into us that social values were important. But I sure had some struggles when it came to our differences about sexual mores. And I still think you made us come home earlier than anybody else!"

I worried about responsibility and ambition. "Even if you do not know where you're going, start someplace," I pleaded to deaf ears. "It doesn't matter what you do, but do the best you can — be the *best* car mechanic, the *best* teacher, the *best* musician." I think I must have drummed that message hard. I remember driving madly to junior high to pick up Ann on her first day after she had dissolved in tears because she thought, quite mistakenly, that she had tested so poorly that she had been relegated to a mediocre homeroom class. When Ann grew up, she became a *good* teacher. And even though Steve hated school so much that he started "dropping out" as early as the first grade, he is a *good* musician. It was a blow when I found out that he genuinely detested the structure of school. He says now that it was "a horrible, frightening, numbing experience," that he was shy to the point of "being stunned" by all of the events around him. "This was the big puzzle," he wrote from college later. "Why did my parents, whom I loved incredibly, send me away when I was so young to an awful place for most of the day and expect me to like it? It didn't make sense."

I worried about the careless way they regarded money and material things. Steve once explained casually that he never asked us for anything — and so he wanted a $500 amplifier for his guitar. Mary Kay thought nothing of buying a sweater that cost as much as George and I used to spend on food for a week. And I often found myself inquiring if the last McGovern to drive the car had gone into the business of collecting secondhand junk.

I worried about dropping out of school, auto accidents, sexual promiscuity, radicalism, apathy, smoking, liquor — and drugs. And as I worried, I tried to understand teen-age turmoil, what was "normal" and what was not, and why so many young people were asking "Who am I?", "What am I?", "Where do I want to go?" I had never been through that.

A few years ago Janet Nichol, the teen-age daughter of good South Dakota friends of ours, Evelyn and Fred Nichol, was killed in an automobile accident. Before her tragic death this is what she wrote about life:

> When I die, I want to be assured that I have really lived this life.
> I want my days to be full of immense suffering and joy.
> I want calm, warm days and cold, lifeless days
> And I want to be able to perceive them.
> To think, and dream and talk, and remain silent.
> When I die, I want to know that my existing has made a difference — a difference in that I have made an influence on many people's lives.
> That I have made them fuller or happier people.
> When I die, I want to know that I haven't wasted a second — that I'm a complete person, have experienced much and understand much.
> What will I be or do? Who knows? . . . It matters, yes . . . but it will come if the rest comes. . .
> When I die . . . perhaps I will die tomorrow.

Of course, Janet's words sum up the dreams of the young; live! feel! experience! reach out beyond what is known to the newer, uncharted path! But often it is a lonely journey, particularly if parents do not understand.

"The young may be envied by their elders," Professor Lawrence Fuchs of Brandeis writes, "but adolescence in America is increasingly a time of acute loneliness. Because the adolescent is self-absorbed in the struggle for identity and intimacy, parents see him as self-centered, unplanned, inefficient, not punctual, and unresponsive — and are often unsympathetic in react-

ing to the turbulence of his feelings. Thus the teen-
ager, ostensibly wanting distance from his parents, gets
it. Parents, not wanting it, find it difficult to close the
gap. When they try, the teen-ager often resents their
intrusion and feels even more alone in his search for
identity and love." When our five children were breaking through adolescence, I know that both George and
I were often unsympathetic because we did not really
understand when rebellion was a healthy searching for
individuality or when it was an unhealthy "acting out."
And we were faced with varying degrees of problems,
some quite serious, such as the arrest of one of our
daughters.

In July 1968 Teresa was arrested in South Dakota
for possession of marijuana. I know this has happened
in many families in recent years, but perhaps our experience was more bizarre than most because it took
place only days before George made the startling announcement, after the death of Robert Kennedy, that
he was going to run as a peace candidate for President
of the United States.

"What is happening to Terry is the only thing in the
world that could make me forget the war," George
confided during one long, miserable night after we had
flown to South Dakota to help her. But he had also
come to me later and mused that perhaps he should
get into national politics "if the country is so mixed up
that even our own daughter is playing with drugs." I
did not have an answer for him. As far as I was concerned, the world was falling apart, yet life was going

on as usual. It seemed paradoxical that Teresa was in deep trouble and that George was about to embark on an unlikely, last-minute Presidential bid — I first heard about his final decision on the television news. What is happening to this family is unreal, I remember thinking.

The national and international events that took place concurrently, before, during, and after the troubled 1968 Democratic Convention, eventually transformed our lives. But during this period of time, in fact for months thereafter, an essential part of me dwelt on the reasons Teresa had felt she needed drugs to cope with the stresses of her adolescence. Before going further I must say that Teresa, a valiant fighter, overcame her difficulties and is now a beautiful, self-reliant young woman. The case against her was dropped because of a legal flaw, and she put her own problems in perspective with the help of therapy. But I still wonder what I could have done as a parent to be more helpful. As it was, I tried to talk to her, sensibly one minute, then berating her the next. Some days I went out in the car looking for her; other days I insisted that I would deny her rights until I was certain she was not using drugs. My fears were all-consuming. "I'll search your room, I'll open your mail, I'll listen to your phone calls," I said, half serious, half bluffing. "I'll do *anything* to keep drugs away from you. I'll not sit by and say, 'Yes, my darling daughter.'" Not long ago, Teresa told me it had been good that I said those things. I still am not sure. "You say you think I could have worked things

----

out better if it had not been for the drugs," she says.
"Maybe that is true. I wanted to be on my own, grown
up, independent. I thought that drugs made it easier
— *then!*"

I do not believe that all young people who use psychedelic drugs are crying for help. But I think
Teresa was, and for reasons only she can fully understand. "We do not see any pattern of causes either in
the social environment or in the families of youngsters
who use drugs excessively," concludes the staff of the
Child Study Association of America. ". . . Whatever
their reasons for using drugs, all youngsters express —
in one way or another — their need for guidance from
their parents and from other adults. They have questions about drugs and about themselves and questions
about the world in which they live."

Quite naturally, my own experience of watching a
child use marijuana and LSD to cope with the unpleas-
ant side effects of life has made me skeptical about the
drug culture. But I will acknowledge that we are in
one. My views coincide with those of Dr. John Buck-
man, an associate professor of psychiatry at the University of Virginia School of Medicine, who says, "The
chemical has become the companion, the panacea but
also the instrument of self-deception and the execu-
tioner. It also had been a means of expression of individual misery and group conflict. We use chemicals to
combat illness, to prolong life, to kill, to promote a
feeling of belonging and also to document the claim of
being different. We use them to proclaim our free-

----

dom and at the same time become slaves. We use them to become more aware and sensitive, but also to numb and to exclude reality. We use them to punish others by provoking guilt, but we also use them to be caught and punished by provoking anger.

"But the use of drugs has other, deeper, more primitive and less well understood meanings. Symbolically the drug is a magical substance, often deeply desired but also feared. It is desired for its nutritious and healing properties because often it reduces pain, hunger, anxiety and anger.

"By the use of forbidden drugs, some of our early fantasies of omnipotence are revived. We are tempted to see 'if we can handle it' — or we play Russian roulette."

It is difficult to know exactly what I would do today if a child of mine was involved with psychedelic or addictive drugs. I think I would try to be more trusting; after all, young people want to survive. And I would listen more carefully; some young people talk about drugs for months before parents realize that they are airing some guilt or are verbalizing an intent. Most assuredly, I would try to avoid focusing on the child involved to the extent of ignoring other family needs; *all* of my family tell me now that I was too "Terry-oriented." I would try to be aware of what Dr. Robert Brown, of Charlottesville, Virginia, called the "panicky parent syndrome" and try to understand, instead, some common stages of reaction: disbelief (my child would never do that!); anger (I'm furious with him!);

panic (I'm helpless to deal with this!); alienation (we cannot communicate any longer!); anxiety (what will this mean in the long run?).

And I would not be a "buddy" to a child taking drugs. Dr. Judianne Densen-Gerber, executive director of Odyssey House centers in New York City, Salt Lake City, Detroit, New Hampshire, Louisiana, and New Jersey — I serve on the board now — told me recently that parents have to set the limits. "If your child persists in using harmful drugs," she warns, "get him to a doctor, a psychiatrist, a family minister, a lawyer, or a counselor with experience. If he is using opiates, you may have to say, 'You can't stay here. I will not support your habit.' Or you may have to take steps to save his life by having him legally incarcerated. The important thing is to *take a position of value*."

When I asked Dr. Densen-Gerber if she would be quite so tough with young people who smoke marijuana, her answer was "no." But until we know more about the long-term effects of that substance, I think we must be as cautious about its use as we are about alcohol. Without question, alcohol is now the most serious drug problem in the United States; yet, curiously, a drinking youngster is more acceptable to most parents than the child who smokes marijuana.

In a society in which at least half of the adult population uses stimulants, depressants, or tranquilizers, we cannot expect our children to be any wiser or more careful about drugs than they are. And things are not going to get better until we spend great amounts of money for research and for rehabilitation of those already damaged by drugs; strengthen laws to penalize those who traffic in narcotics; and educate our adolescents, already trying to break through the most stressful period in their young lives, to the dangers of pot, hash, LSD, amphetamines, barbiturates, opiates, liquor, and other drugs on the lethal list. Many of us, too many of us, can look around within the framework of family and friends and see those games of "Russian roulette." And the stakes are very high.

Chapter VIII

1968

W<small>HEN</small> G<small>EORGE</small> <small>SAID</small> to me, "What is happening to Terry is the only thing in the world that could make me forget the war," he was not being melodramatic. It is difficult to explain how genuinely passionate we both felt — and still feel — about that war. From August 2, 1963, when he was the first to rise on the Senate floor and challenge our entanglement in Vietnam, the war became, as described by Robert Anson, George's "magnificent obsession." And it was mine too.

My recollections of those angry, bitter years flash in close-ups and dialogue: a scene in a ward at Walter Reed Army Hospital, where I went with Steve and the boys in his combo to entertain and to visit with maimed young veterans only a few months older than they, but without feet or legs — a vision underscored by

George's admonition, "I'm fed up with old men dreaming up wars for young men to die in"; images of the branding accusations in letters from constituents, inflammatory attacks questioning George's patriotism, calling forth his quiet reply, "To remain silent in the face of policies we believe to be wrong is not patriotism; it is moral cowardice, a form of treason to one's conscience and to the nation. It is not easy to dissent in time of war. I do not know how all this will come out. I do know that the people of a state can easily secure a new Senator, but a Senator cannot easily secure a new conscience." And engraved in my mind are the details on the floor of the Senate while the disappointing 39–55 vote was polled against the McGovern-Hatfield bill to cut off war funds, the Senators bent over their desks, an etching in a history book, animated by my husband's charging with such ardor that tremors ran up my spine, "It doesn't take courage at all for a Congressman or a Senator or a President to wrap himself in the flag and say we're staying in Vietnam! Because it isn't our blood that is being shed! But we are responsible for those young men and their lives and hopes. And if we don't end this foolish, damnable war, those young men will someday curse us for our pitiful willingness to let the Executive carry the burden the Constitution put on us."

I fervently shared George's conviction, but not his courage. Many times I wondered if he might not be throwing his future down the drain with no assurance that his stand made any difference at all.

The future, as it turned out, was shaped by other forces, in particular the assassination of Robert Kennedy. George and Robert Kennedy liked and respected each other. In fact, it was Bob who first suggested in 1967 — before Eugene McCarthy was approached to take the job — that George was the right person to be a peace candidate, an idea then rejected because it would preclude our Senatorial race back home. Again, months later, during the long ride back from New York to Arlington Cemetery on the funeral train bearing Bob's body, in spite of our reluctance to think about political plans when we were numb with sadness, the subject was broached again. And in the following weeks, in those surrealistic early-summer days during which our country suffered shock after shock, the pressure mounted for George to keep together Bob's delegates to the Convention. Realistically, he did not have a chance to win the nomination. But he had the hope that he might be able to help secure adoption of a platform that would hasten peace in Vietnam. And he had a strong memory of a friend with courage.

Two months before he was shot, Bob Kennedy had gone to South Dakota to campaign for the Presidential nomination — and to help George in his forthcoming Senate race. While there he had said this: "There is no one I feel more genuinely about, whether we are in politics together or not — about the importance of his contribution and the importance of his understanding and feeling — than George McGovern. Of all my colleagues in the U.S. Senate, the person who has the most feeling and does things in the most genuine way, without affecting his life, is George McGovern. He is so highly admired by his colleagues, not just for his ability but because of the kind of man he is. That is truer of him than of any man in the U.S. Senate."

George's response was that Bob Kennedy had the qualifications to be one of our great Presidents. "I have heard all the talk about his ruthlessness and his long hair," he said with affection, "but he isn't as ruthless as the great Theodore Roosevelt and his hair isn't half as long as Thomas Jefferson's, and, unlike Abraham Lincoln, he has no beard at all. What he does have is the absolute personal honesty of Woodrow Wilson, the stirring passion for leadership of Andrew Jackson, and the profound acquaintance with personal tragedy of Lincoln."

One last time after this exchange Bob went back to South Dakota to campaign in his Presidential primary and George took him to the airport. "I remember that morning being seized with a feeling of sadness," recalls George. "For some reason he looked so small. Bob, at various times, appeared different sizes to me. Sometimes he looked like a large man, I mean physically. At other times he seemed very slight, small. But as he walked away, he looked frail, and stooped, and tired. And he seemed just kind of wistful about the whole thing. I just had such a feeling of sadness as he got on the plane that day, and a kind of feeling that he was a lonely figure."

I have seen that loneliness in many public men; in fact, I think it is there in all. But we ask too much from them that is superficial and we tend to turn away their efforts to tap any latent ability in us. We want our leaders to lead, but not to ask too much of us personally. Then we are dissatisfied because we feel marginal in government. We feel empty because we are detached and not in control of our own destiny. Yet we do not expend the effort it takes to gain a greater measure of control. It is a depressing cycle. Still, somehow the overpowering urge to lead, the recurrent optimism that the best in people will catch fire, keeps some politicians going against all the odds. It was that way with Bob Kennedy. It has been that way with George.

The morning after I had heard on the TV news about George's candidacy, the whole family dressed up and drove to Capitol Hill for a press conference. It was August 10, just sixteen days before the Democrats were to convene in Chicago to weigh the nomination of Hubert Humphrey or Eugene McCarthy and, now, George. The children and I had to be there, of course, not to answer questions, but to show our support, and I dreaded it and felt awkward seated behind the long, cold table facing the crowd in the Senate Caucus Room.

George began: "I bring no claim to the Kennedy mantle, but I believe deeply in the twin goals for which Robert Kennedy gave his life — an end to the war in

Vietnam and a passionate commitment to heal the divisions in our own society . . ." I could not concentrate on the words he had written the night before in our little paneled den. I had never been close to so many cameras, microphones, cables, so much *metal*. And I was astonished by the number of reporters who had showed up on a hot Saturday morning. "Just as brotherhood is the condition of survival in a nuclear world, so it is the condition of peace in America . . . It is for these purposes that I declare myself a candidate for the Presidential nomination," George concluded. And the next thing I knew, he and his aides sailed out of the room, leaving behind in the noise and confusion, like lambs in slaughter season, our inexperienced family. Then the national press corps converged, some jostling and shoving the others to be near Teresa, shouting at me such questions as, "Why is your husband running?" "Do you think he has a chance?" "What about your daughter's arrest? How did it happen?" "Why did she turn to drugs?" and "What will happen?" It was bedlam.

When we got home, I changed into grubby garden clothes and shoes caked with mud and went for a ride. I had been inarticulate, I knew, but I could not have been more put off by the sudden personal nature of the questions by the press, or more frozen with anger for having been left defenseless by the staff. Why hadn't somebody warned me, shielded Teresa, protected poor Mary Kay and Steve? Why was I feeling at bay about my role as a wife, deemed both essential and

expendable, quotable yet unqualified to offer substan-
tive observations, neither a valid reflection of my husband nor quite a total person without him? How could
I explain in words the meld of affection, pride, and
perplexity I felt for George, or my mixed emotions
about what he was doing? Ellen Proxmire, before her
divorce, warned forthrightly that a Senator's wife
"must try to learn control without erasing completely
the possibility of honest emotion. It is so easy in the
world of politics to be hysterical about everything
— about your chances, about your opposition, about
the press, about cranks who write and demand the
impossible, about the frequent unfairness of it all."
That was it: it was unfair; but, no, in all honesty, it was
not.

When I turned into our driveway, reporters and
cameramen were sprinkled over the yard, spilling onto
the next-door lawn that Hubert had tended so carefully before he had become Vice President and had
moved into a high-rise apartment downtown. I did
not want to think about him or about the time that had
intervened since the four of us had closed all discussion about the war in Vietnam. Rather, I would take a
lesson from Muriel, my unassuming, constrained good
friend, who had learned to camouflage paralyzing anxiety in order to meet the public and the press with
grace. She would have understood my trepidation that
day about a television interview — the first I had ever
had — which ended up poorly after I rushed to my
bedroom to run a comb through my hair and change

into a dress, then paused for deep, deep breaths at the top of the stairs, and finally marched straight to the cameras and up to Bob Goralski, without a glimmer of an idea what I was going to say, still wearing muddy gardening shoes. I remember dimly that Ila was at the foot of the stairs watching all of this, with tears streaming down her face. I never found time to ask her why.

That was the opening of a slapstick-comedy week, a time I might have enjoyed if my heart had not been heavy about Teresa. At first, Ila and a friend, Colleen Jacques, handled things. Then the Secret Service arrived, sprouting like toadstools in the rose garden, in the basement, on the side porch — a lot of them, including a special detail for George and one for me headed by a jovial young man named Barney Boyett. I sent the children to market and did not have my hair done because I felt ridiculous dragging those men along. Then Mary Hoyt, a writer who had handled radio and television for the Peace Corps, appeared in the living room, a stranger, but comfortably compatible. Her job was to help me help myself. How could I contribute but not look foolish in Chicago? How could we best handle the question of Teresa's arrest? Who could we ask to throw together a last-minute Women for McGovern organization? What about the engraved invitations to a tea Shirley MacLaine would give to introduce the family to delegates? Where could I find a couple of appropriate dresses for color TV? And, most particularly, how would I budget my time with the media?

Even before Mary arrived to take over George's desk in the den, she called with advice; for example, she offered, some of the more aggressive press, say, the *Women's Wear Daily* reporter, wouldn't let a thing slip by, so it might be best to postpone interviews until things were under control. "It's too late," I moaned. *"Women's Wear* is at the door!" It had not occurred to me to see the reporter at *my* convenience. That is why my first interview as a national candidate's wife, my first interview in a national publication, and my first chat with controversial Kandy Stroud, who writes gossip for the "Beautiful People," described me as wide-eyed and awash in a "tiny brick and white clapboard" home that was "teeming with collies, a Siamese cat named Sam, a tiny black kitten, an assortment of birds, and an assortment of teen-agers" — drying my hair in pink and yellow rollers with a portable hair dryer!

Flying to Chicago on our own chartered propjet Electra filled with family and friends and press, headed toward we knew not what, was like giving a party that was slightly out of control. By that time there were jokes about our little staff being the "ruthless McGovern machine" and George had told reporters that by "announcing when we did, we have at least eliminated the possibility of peaking early." Jauntiness was not entirely a façade; it helped to support the reality that it was too late to get into the picture without a miracle and too late to pull out without letting down some stalwart Democrats.

At Chicago's Sheraton-Blackstone Hotel campaign headquarters had been set up hurriedly, the command post largely in the living room of our small one-bedroom suite with its fourth-floor view overlooking Michigan Avenue, Grant Park, and the Hilton Hotel, so close to the color and noise that we were hypnotically drawn to the windows to watch the carnival street scene below: clusters of girls in white boater hats, banded in red, white, and blue; youngsters in blue jeans and tattered hair, salting their way through little bands of delegates in shirt sleeves and bright cotton dresses, their credentials prominently displayed; brassy bands playing "Happy Days" and kids with bullhorns and angry voices; and sirens that cut a swath in the air, heralding another candidate's motorcade, another heat-stroke victim, another confrontation between an antiwar demonstrator and a cop.

The living room of the suite was for strategy sessions, for the ebb and flow of politicians, delegates, speech writers, movie stars; for Abe Ribicoff, Arthur Schlesinger, Ted Sorenson, Stewart Udall, Henry Kimelman; for trays of hamburgers and watery Scotches and baskets of scratch-paper speech drafts; for South Dakotans with tears and kisses; for Gloria Steinem with a headful of ideas and a bag of money collected from supporters; and for Frank Mankiewicz and Pierre Salinger and other former Kennedy staff people who appeared and got right on the telephones. The adjoining room, a visual disaster with an extra rollaway bed and two big wing chairs taking up all space not littered with French fries, odd shoes, and overflow guests, was headquarters for me and the family.

By the summer of 1968 our family had increased by two sons-in-law, Jim Rowen and Wilbur Mead. Sue and Jim had been married at home in Washington. I can still see her gliding down the stairs, taking her vows in the living room which was filled with greens and balalaika music. Then at the reception on Capitol Hill we all danced — I wondered if it had been done before — in the elegant old Senate Dining Room, transformed with potted palms. Ann and Wilbur's wedding a few months later was equally sentimental but every bit as different as the girls are. Ann was a rosy-cheeked bride in white in a formal church ceremony in Mitchell. I had driven out to South Dakota accompanied only by our collie, Mara, to prepare for the five hundred guests, old friends, dear family. For me it was a nostalgic time, a slightly melancholy interlude during which I thought about the family growing up. Then I got so bogged down with details that I did not have time to have my hair done before the ceremony. I told both my girls that I could not have picked out sons-in-law I loved more.

The biggest problem in having the family at the convention with us, plus Ila and her brood, and George's sisters and their husbands, and my friend Colleen Jacques and her children, was logistical. No one was quite sure where to sleep or how to keep in touch — an increasingly frantic situation as each incredible day progressed. And the children were never quite sure whether they were going to be barred from the suite because nobody recognized them, or caught unexpectedly for interviews by the national press. At one time or another it was reported that Sue had said, *"No one* expects her father to be nominated for President," and that Teresa had said, "People will separate the political from the *personal* situation," and that Mary Kay was a miserable, exploited child. At least that was the narration on a dramatic television documentary on a major network, showing a crazy picture of our little twelve-year-old with her face screwed up in pain. Here was a child in personal anguish because her father wanted to be President, the commentary indicated, when in actuality Mary Kay had been photographed on stage at her father's arrival press conference in Chicago, suffering from an itchy heat rash and a sore head caused by a stray wire from TV equipment that had somehow snagged her scalp, but grimacing bravely because there wasn't anything else to do about her physical discomfort. We were amazed at the off-target observation about her and wished the network had talked to her before editorializing.

It seemed to me that within an hour after we arrived at the Blackstone George was hopelessly behind schedule, the children were bored and restless, the bedroom was a mess, and I was riveted to a wing chair in anxiety. Mary Hoyt had called a full-scale press conference for me at eleven the next morning on the grounds that it would be impossible to talk to many members of the media individually. Besides, as the candidate's wife, a well-worn title that had overnight assumed considerable weight and patina, I was suddenly newsworthy. But I had already said everything there was to say about George's announcement. Also, I had never had a formal press conference called just for me.

What I wanted to do most was to talk about George's sincerity; I had even decided to keep repeating my description of him as "a gentle man with a spine of steel." Yet Mary, wearing her press-secretary hat, convinced me that if I did not reveal something of myself voluntarily, I would probably have to respond to questions I might not be willing to answer. And so the two of us, huddled in the wing chairs in the corner of the bedroom, ignoring the commotion around us, weighed the offensive versus the defensive approach. I had already told a reporter in Washington that I was cowardly, shy, and usually kept quiet because I was not the Senator, George was. But those words printed in the newspaper seemed out of character and quite unlike anything I had ever said or thought. Still, would anybody care about views formulated from such ordinary experiences as living on a farm, raising children, or reading good books? Yes, Mary insisted, that is exactly what they want to know.

The next morning nine of us — the children and Ila and I — threaded our way through reporters and camera crews in a ballroom of the Blackstone. Before the elevator doors opened I worried that nobody would be there. Then when I saw the rows of relatively quiet, serious-looking press women — and men — I worried because they were. But, once I began, it was no worse than debating on stage at Woonsocket High. First, I addressed myself to the generation gap, about which I felt qualified to speak. "It's a bad habit," I announced bravely. "One of the things I'd like to do is bring about a healing of the divisions." I was afraid this sounded like pie-in-the-sky political rhetoric, but I wanted to say something constructive about the creativity and idealism of the young people who were being so cynically maligned in 1968. "The most idealistic in the long run is often the most realistic," I said then, and I have repeated it many times since. Then I slipped in a plug for libraries, perhaps one of the lowest priority issues ever discussed at a national political convention. And finally I brought my monologue to a close by commenting on the migration to the cities, saying, "I love the land. It's part of my heritage. We must find a way for people to stay on the land." It was hard for me to gauge the reaction of the press, although I felt surprisingly confident that I was taken seriously. Mary reported later that she had turned to Dr. Lawn Thompson, our family physician — it is traditional to have a doctor in a candidate's entourage — and whispered, "She's surprising them," and he had answered, "She's surprising *herself!*" It was quite true.

For the next few days I spent a lot of time pegging along in high heels beside George as he raced from hotel to hotel, the last-minute candidate, eager to visit as many state convention delegates as the staff and his long-time personal secretary, Pat Donovan, could set up. There were confusing, on-the-spot changes, which sometimes took place en route. The streets were like a furnace; the caucus rooms, icy cold. I do not remember being tired, only so lame that we purloined from room service an enormous silver tureen filled with crushed ice so that I could soak my feet while I had private time in the suite or when I was being interviewed.

What I was going to wear for those media interviews became a problem of ridiculous proportions. I cannot imagine burning up so much energy in that way today. Shortly before appearing on NBC, for instance, after Mary had discovered that the interviewer, Aline Saarinen, and I were dressed in the same color, we searched madly until we found Ann, who was wearing *the* good red dress in the family, then quickly switched outfits. I was curious about women like the late Mrs. Saarinen, women in the media with national reputations. But it was impossible to know what to expect from them, particularly after Betty Beale of the Washington *Star* had been seriously interested in whether George snored, and Elizabeth Shelton of the Washington *Post* had called long distance to ask if the Secret Service would let a photographer take pictures of our pets, then wrote a story that included a mention of our unnamed canary. I remember wondering why Charlotte Curtis of the *New York Times*, whose reputation for wit and acerbity preceded her, wanted to tag along with me to a "Gala Tribute to Muriel," an enormous musical extravaganza for my old neighbor, an event I dreaded as much as anything I had ever been expected to attend. I suspected that my sickening feeling of reluctance to remind Muriel in any way of the unspoken tension between us was apparent; if it was, Charlotte did not make light of it. Instead, after we arrived at the hotel where the huge party was being held, she and Mary took me directly to the hotel manager's office and left me there with two Secret Service agents while they worked their way through the crush of Democratic women in the ballroom, and then came back in full agreement that there were hundreds there and I need not attend because nobody, especially Muriel, would even be able to see me. And it is funny to recall the tension that mounted before George and I met Barbara Walters for an appearance on the "Today" show. For me, nervousness was brought on to some degree by a note Mary had hastily scrawled, suggesting that for interviews in general I might wish to smile more and give briefer answers, but for Barbara I should be prepared for "more thoughtful, elaborate thinking." I still have that note to remind me that Barbara's one question was this: "Where did your son, Steve, spend the night?", an embarrassing point of concern that George and I had been discussing when we walked into the studio, an hour or two before we ascertained that he had spent the night in Grant Park with Colleen's son, Jack Jacques. (After we left the studio that morning, as our motorcade pulled up to the front of the Blackstone, I looked out of the limousine

----

window and saw two staunch little figures, Mary Kay
and Mary Beth Jacques, standing on the corner curb
trying to pass out McGovern literature to delegates.
They admitted later that they had also been surrepti-
tiously pasting McGovern bumper stickers across the
huge McCarthy for President paper flowers that
bloomed across the city.)

As is usually the case at a convention, there was a
luncheon for the candidates' wives and Democratic
"women doers." This one found me seated at the head
table high above hundreds of women, miserably sure
that any friends would be pitying me and any enemies
would be eyeing the McGovern family table, at which
Teresa's chair was vacant until she found courage to
face the crowd right before dessert was served. Afterward there was a fashion show reflecting the eras of
former First Ladies — from Dolly Madison to Jacque-
line Kennedy — that prompted the ample-sized Mrs.
Richard Hughes, wife of the former governor of New
Jersey, to tell a story that Abigail McCarthy recounts
in her book *Private Faces, Public Places.* "That
Eleanor," Betty Hughes evidently said. "I remember
her at Atlantic City. She came to rehearse for the style
show and kept saying that the size fives were slipping
right off her. I said to my secretary, 'Let's drown her
in the punch bowl!' "

The other memorable social event was the tea that
Shirley MacLaine hosted for me and the children, ostensibly to mark the opening of a "hospitality suite,"
our contribution to the social life of the delegates, far

less interesting than the glittering dinners and musicals for Muriel and Hubert, and the fifty buffet dinners in private homes of liberal Democrats for Abigail and Gene. Again, before the elevator doors opened into the same huge area where the press conference had been held, now converted into a hospitality suite, I prayed that somebody would be there. On one side of the room was Muriel, who had walked across the street to wish me well, accompanied by a contingent of press and her son, Bobby, and his wife, who were hugging their old friends, Sue and Jim, and sharing with them a wedding anniversary cake. Knowing our old neighbors were now competitors, I had a lump in my throat, but I concentrated on introducing people to each other. Even at that point I was naive enough to think that it was supposed to be a *real tea,* not another excuse for press coverage.

On the other side of the room people were stacked around Shirley, who was radiantly discussing Vietnam, law and order, the democratic process, the excess war profits tax, and the fact that she and 173 other California delegates were still exhilarated over George's hugely successful debate that morning with Hubert and Gene. It had been a triumph for George. Most of the family had gone along, slipping into the back of a caucus room in the LaSalle Hotel, jammed with spectators and reporters and television crews. I had known that it was going to be difficult for George to debate the war with Hubert and to face Gene after George had been reported as saying, "Well, Gene doesn't really want to be President, and I do." Gene had started right out defending himself against any suggestion that he might not be a President active enough to solve America's problems at home as well as abroad. He was debonair, as usual, but his speech was not met with much enthusiasm. Then Hubert had taken over the microphone and said, "I did not come here to repudiate the President of the United States. I want that made quite clear," and dovish delegates, interpreting that to mean he would not change Lyndon Johnson's foreign policy, hissed and booed. Then George got up and spoke, carefully, without rancor, about war and racism and poverty, and as the delegates clapped and cheered approvingly, he relaxed and became even more eloquent. Afterward just about everybody agreed that he had been firm and graceful — the winner.

George and I hardly had a chance to speak to each other in Chicago, certainly never alone. Even after the suite cleared out in the early-morning hours, there was the rubble to throw away, and the bedroom was like a dormitory, with Steve or Mary Kay or their cousin Bobby Pennington on the rollaway bed. I did not even try to keep up with the news, to interpret snatches of political gossip, to react to well-meaning friends who brought little leaps of hope or dispensed outrageous stories about the ugliness and obscenity that was swelling into a mushroom cloud over Grant Park. About all I could do was to hold up for George, and he was very

tough with me that week about keeping up a good
front. "I know it's hard for all of you," he said to me
once. "But there are still people with hope, and we
cannot let them down." I was all right until Wednes-
day afternoon, when I stayed in the suite to watch on
television the fate of the minority plank, the peace
plank. When the vote was 1567 for the majority and
only 1041 for the minority, I wept. It was all over for
our people, and even going through the motions of
putting George's name into nomination seemed ridiculous. I was so crushed and bitter that George held me
in his arms for a few minutes and gently reminded me
that we had to play out the script. Late that afternoon
I noticed two of our finest young volunteers, Paul
Moore, Jr., and Tom Kenworthy, heading toward the
park. They had changed from quiet street clothes into
their blue jeans and had tied black bands on their
arms. And, although I did not know it then, Steve and
Teresa left the hotel too and joined the others mourn-
ing for peace in a candlelight parade.

The children and I were hastily dressing to go to
Convention Hall for George's formal nomination —
the candidates themselves do not appear at Convention Hall until after the voting has been completed —
when the tear gas started leaking through the windows
of the suite. All afternoon trouble had been heating
up across the street in Grant Park. From our window
the transformation was eerie. No longer were the
young people frozen into a kind of mass audience; now
they were running in packs, marching in twos and

threes, pairing off, scattering behind the trees, to be replaced by columns of blue-helmeted policemen. And suddenly Barney and Mary were pounding on the door to say that we had to leave immediately or not go at all.

None of us was quite sure what to be afraid of, but we were afraid. Downstairs, in the gas-filled streets, we crowded ourselves into a limousine that took off almost before the doors were closed. As we looked back through the rear window, it appeared as though the crowd on Michigan Avenue was going to break like a wave over the car. But our police-escorted motorcade wheeled off through the city streets, out onto the freeway, and up to Convention Hall, where another drama was being enacted.

Sometimes I look at a newspaper picture of me and the children taken that night, standing in our box overlooking the convention floor, smiling, clapping, seeming full of pride and joy. And it makes me feel like a fraud. I cannot imagine at what point that photograph was shot. I do know that one of my significant emotions came from the dramatic, stunning moment when Abe Ribicoff stopped right in the middle of nominating George to say, "With George McGovern we wouldn't have Gestapo tactics on the streets of Chicago!" Then he looked balefully at Mayor Daley and said, "How hard it is to accept the truth! How hard it is!" I was also moved by reports relayed by Mary and Barney, who were crouched on the floor of our box, out of sight, listening to Barney's Secret Service radio-

phone news that indicated that everything was dangerously out of control back in the hotel area; and from
the sight of Sue, weeping when she heard about kids
being bludgeoned, her head bent forward so that her
long, dark hair hid her face; and Jim, close to tears too.
My emotions were not pride and joy that night. All I
wanted was to be back at the hotel with George.

There, in the center of the chaos of the suite, I
found him, pacing back and forth in front of the television set. The windows were open and the curtains
flapped in the breeze and the acrid smell of tear gas
still hung in the air. George was pale with shock and I
had never seen him so angry. He had been watching
from the windows and he had seen the police beat a
young antiwar demonstrator to the ground, then drag
him away by the heels. And another girl, a McGovern
worker, who had volunteered to carry a message across
the street to the Hilton, had been hit by a police trun-
cheon. Those who had been overlooking the melee
could not stop telling what it had been like. "The police poured out of National Guard trucks and lined up
with drawn rifles. It was a military attack!" Pat Donovan said desperately. "The Senator kept going from
window to window. I don't think he caught half of his
own nomination speech." We stayed up late talking
about what the riots meant. The children were indignant; George was heartsick; and I too spent to reach
out.

The next day at a press conference George said this:
"When young people or old people or people of any

age assemble to peacefully protest policies over which they have no voice, it seems to me that it is well within the American constitutional system. I don't come here to encourage lawlessness, but I do remind you that this country began with the Boston Tea Party, and I think what happened out on Michigan Avenue was a case of police power getting out of hand."

The children all agree that their memories of the convention are heavy with anger and sadness. Steve, for example, says that he knew his dad was not going to be nominated, but he was glad that he had gone to Chicago. Nevertheless, he had been anxious, even afraid, and he had wanted to stay in the park. "They tried to keep me out of the hotel. I remember I got weird looks just because I was young," he recalls, "and when I wanted to buy cigarettes, the storekeeper slammed the door in my face and locked it." Sue and Jim and Ann and Wilbur say they knew they had to stay with us, with "the establishment," because George was a prominent public figure. But they did not like it. The whole family admits to breaking down when the filmed documentary of Robert Kennedy's life was shown. They all remember the hate-filled woman behind Mary Kay and Teresa who threatened to pour hot coffee down Teresa's back when she joined others singing a sustained, emotional chorus of "The Battle Hymn of the Republic."

I doubt if any Democrat attending the 1968 convention will ever forget the shame or the subsequent soul-searching about why the violence took place. It was a turning point for the party, we know that much, and I happen to think it marked the end of boss politics. It was also more complicated than that: there was a cultural gap between the so-called "hippie-radicals" and the so-called "law and order pigs"; there was a rebellion on the part of the younger faction against all authority; above all, there was the war, the bleak and senseless killing that had been thrust upon too many unwilling young humans. It was all of these — and more — that fanned the violence. I felt certain then that revulsion against fighting in Vietnam was the strongest common denominator, but now I have a slightly different perspective. "As we make people powerless," Rollo May says, "we promote their violence rather than its control. Deeds of violence in our society are performed largely by those trying to establish their self-esteem, to defend their self-image, and to demonstrate that they, too, are significant." In the case of the Chicago disgrace perhaps this principle should be applied to both the young people and the police before any conclusions are drawn.

It was on just this subject that Muriel and I took opposite points of view when we met privately after Hubert had been nominated. Late in the afternoon on the day he was choosing his running mate, she came to call. The children and Mary and I had collapsed across the unmade beds, oblivious of the litter all over the room, quietly talking about events in the preceding hours, when Betty South, Muriel's press secretary, called to say they were on their way from across the street. My first impulse was to giggle. Muriel had seen things almost as bad at my house before. Yet it had been a long time since we had been informal and intimate.

By the time she arrived, Mary had single-handedly moved the steel folding bed into the hall — the Secret Service agent guarding my door watched sympathetically but said it was against rules for him to help with any "personal" tasks — and had thrown George's socks into the closet, stuffed the newspapers in the bathroom, and ordered tea and little cakes. Meanwhile, I had placated the children, who were furious about being roused, changed into one of Sue's dresses — she was wearing one of mine — fixed up my face, and curled up in the wing chair by the window.

It was just like Muriel to think of those in defeat even at the same time that Hubert, in her words, "was over there agonizing in his bathrobe about a Vice-Presidential candidate." I learned later that she went to visit Abigail too. It was a strong, warm gesture I shall not forget. But it is one of the ironies of life that often friends grow apart, especially in political life, and it is difficult to accept that fact. It is strange how often over the years Muriel and I have been destined to be in the same pattern, our lives touching periodically. I am sure that the circumstances have often been as difficult for my Midwest friend as they have been for me.

The next day we packed up and headed for the airport. George took a plane to South Dakota and the children and I flew back to Washington to close up the house before we drove across the miles to join him. In my last interview in Chicago I told a reporter that I thought George was the only Democratic politician who had come out of the convention better off than he went in. "If it was worthwhile," I observed about what he had done, "I am sure something concrete will come out of this. Many people have told me they feel uplifted and more hopeful because they have another man whom they can turn to as a leader." I believed that, and in my heart I knew that George had already picked up the challenge.

But there was no time to reflect. It was already the end of August, and we had heavy weeks of campaigning ahead to re-elect George to the Senate, without question the right forum for him if he was going to continue in national politics.

Chapter IX

`` *. . . A Time to Build Up"*

IN NOVEMBER 1968 George was re-elected to the Senate, capturing 57 per cent of the vote from his opponent, Archie Gubbrud, a two-term governor, who
brought up again the radical label that others had tried
to pin on George before, indirectly tying that charge to
the "hippie" demonstrations in Chicago. But South
Dakotans were proud of George, I think particularly
because he had had the fortitude to put himself on the
line about the war. On election night, when he acknowledged victory, George quoted from the Bible
verse in Ecclesiastes: "To every thing there is a season,
and a time to every purpose under the heaven . . . A
time of war, and a time of peace." The thought was
unspoken between us, but I knew that until there was
peace the time was coming when George would run for
President again.

Almost immediately after the election invitations flooded his office, particularly from college students, asking him to speak about Vietnam, and he began crisscrossing the United States on a lonely caring mission, giving up almost all of his weekends and Congressional recesses to explain his antiwar rationale. Once in a while I went with him. In Denver in early 1970, when he first struck a theme, "Come Home, America," later used throughout the campaign in 1972, I myself saw a room full of regular Democrats so moved by his words that their eyes glistened. Some wrote their names on little slips of paper, or gave George their cards, or asked him to keep in touch as he laid future plans. This happened all over the country. I shall always admire him for those weary months, when he traveled alone, kept up his own spirits, and buoyed the hopes of a scattered few supporters.

On the bright side, fees from some of the lectures added enough to our income so that we started looking for a new house. I liked our modest home in Chevy Chase, but the yard was no longer a challenge, and even the basement had been renovated and redecorated — George had had it fixed up as a surprise one summer when I was visiting in South Dakota because I had longed for my own private "mess room" (it turned out to be much too nice for that). George had grown impatient about the time it took to drive from Chevy Chase to Capitol Hill or to National Airport; besides, the family had begun to scatter. Ann and Wilbur were in South Dakota, where she was teaching and he was

going back to school after service in the Marines; Sue
and her husband, Jim, were attending the University
of Wisconsin, living in an apartment where the names
on the door, "Jim and Sue," reflected her feminist
leanings; Steve and Mary Kay were in high school; and
Teresa was working and going to school in Charlottesville, Virginia. One day we discovered a modern, Jap-
anese-style house, nestled down below a winding road
in Northwest Washington, surrounded by old trees,
each room so much a part of the landscape that the
outdoors was practically in our laps. I could breathe in
this openness; I could expand in this light, gracious
gem of a house; and I loved it instantly. When we
moved, however, Mary Kay and Steve said that taking
them away from their school and their friends was the
worst thing we had ever done. And so we acquired a
second-hand car and paid the tuition fees required in
Maryland for out-of-state pupils, hoping it would give
them a little bit of continuity, certainly not because we
were prejudiced about the racial and economic inequi-
ties in the District of Columbia school system, as was
suggested later in the Presidential primaries by one ad-
versary.

I had time for my books again. Night after night,
while George was on the road, I tucked myself into a
big chair overlooking the shadowy woods behind our
house, and studied textbooks and magazines and research papers concerned with early childhood development. I was fascinated by the theory that parents
often give too little to young babies — *unknowingly.*

And the more I read, and questioned my own short-comings as a parent, the more concerned I became. I was not worrying about those mistakes I had unwittingly made in raising my family; rather, I wanted to understand the reasons for the differences between those children who are nurtured with special developmental skills and those who are raised more routinely.

I remembered keenly the lack of practical knowledge I had had when I was a young mother. At one point, when Ann and Sue and Teresa were small, I had briefly joined a mothers' club and had attended monthly meetings to talk to a "counselor" about children. My concern then — a relatively minor one, I thought — was that I could not seem to get the little girls to finish anything they started, and the counselor pointedly asked if I had such a tendency myself. Somehow that did not clear up the problem. Only in retrospect do I see that I was too impatient, too bogged down with chores. Today I am acutely conscious of the need to give my grandsons a little more space between the time I suggest that a task be completed and the time I expect it to be done. It seems like such a logical way to teach a child about responsibility, scarcely worth joining a club to learn. But young mothers need help. In my case, being a part of a little group illuminated merely the fact that my worries were not unique.

One day, at the suggestion of my friend Dr. Robert Brown, of the University of Virginia School of Medicine — one of the many doctors with whom I was dis-

cussing recent findings about children — I visited Mrs.
Ruth Rucker, the director of the Parent-Child Center
in Washington, a federally and locally funded experimental project offering practical training for mothers
of infants and young children in Washington, D.C.'s
inner city. Mrs. Rucker is an innovator helping to
transform the black community around the Parent-
Child Center. She told me about the good things that
were happening in that area because local parents were
more involved with their children. There seemed to
be a cycle, she said: Improve the home environment,
and almost inevitably thereafter improvements in the
community in which the youngsters are growing up
start taking place. If I wanted to see for myself, Mrs.
Rucker told me, I could train to be a Family Education
Assistant, a person who goes into homes to teach
mothers the most rudimentary rules of parenting:
how to hold a baby, play with him, stimulate his learning abilities, help him grow emotionally and intellec-
tually.

I went to work on one of the teams. The very first
woman we worked with changed right before our eyes.
Initially she treated her baby boy like a doll, an object
to be fed and dressed up, simply because he was there.
Learning about the need for a "creative environment"
was news to her, even suspect. She was desultory, lethargic, and watched blandly while the other Family Education Assistant and I taught her little boy to play.
There was a healthy response from the child, absolutely none from the mother. But we went back week

after week, and one day she was at the door before we knocked, impatiently waiting to tell us about the skill with which her son was stacking blocks, about his progress in picking out various colors, about his new, more outgoing personality, for which she felt lovingly responsible. Nourished by the new role of mother and teacher, soon she acquired a high school equivalency diploma. She is now a Family Education Assistant herself.

During this period of volunteering for work that stimulated in me more curiosity than it satisfied, in those months preceding George's announcement that he was going to run for the Presidency, I decided that the future of children would be an issue for which I would campaign. As I was to say later, time and time again, "we dishonor the mystery of human life by ignoring children. If a child is properly nourished, learns to love and be loved, to relate to people, to have self-control, he will have a rich future in store. But he learns his value systems early, before the age of five, and that is when he needs a secure sense of himself in order to develop his full potential. That is when he learns right from wrong. Why wait until a child is in trouble before we pay attention to him?"

I simply assumed that the character of our future society — what our children *become* — would be regarded as a central responsibility by most adult citizens. As Eunice Shriver once told me, "In a compassionate society, those with the greatest gifts have the greatest responsibilities for sharing those gifts. Those with the least capacity to sustain themselves are entitled to the most we can provide for their sustenance." In other words, every child, whole or flawed, has rights. I did not realize until later that this subject would put a lot of people to sleep!

In 1972 the rare moments of interest in my views about adult-child relationships came usually when I recounted personal, family stories, such as one about the time our first grandson, Timmy Mead, was born. When Ann had called and told me that she was pregnant, my heart sank. "How foolish!" I scolded, in much the same tone that Dad had used twenty-five years before with me. "You have a fine teaching position that you enjoy, and Wilbur is still in school. How on earth do you expect to manage?" Ann had been shocked by my reaction. "Mother, you're the very last person on earth I expected to say that." Later, while trying to analyze my foolishly negative attitude, I had thought about my own white-haired grandmothers, and, as always, the memories were replete with affection and tenderness and gratitude. But my grandmothers were *old,* or so it had seemed to me. I was not ready to assume a grandparent's role. But by the time Timmy was born, the whole family was ecstatic. Even a sprinkling of friends showed up at the hospital to wait with us until Ann was wheeled out of the delivery room with a blond, blue-eyed infant. I could not wait to touch him, hold him, love him. Almost imperceptibly, I felt his new presence strengthening our family solidarity. He belonged to all of us. And I had been so dazed that I bounced up to a young woman in the hall, reached out to her, and said, "You must be Sue and Jim's friend. Let me introduce myself. *I am Ann McGovern!*" I am sure I said that for many reasons. Birth is a most indescribably joyous event for me, and I obviously wished that I myself had given life to Timmy. But perhaps even more significant was the oneness I felt with my own first-born, Ann. We were truly sharing our womanhood. I think that a time of birth can provide the ultimate closeness for a mother and her daughter.

When the time came for George to announce his candidacy for the Democratic Presidential nomination, he and I did not really weigh his chances or analyze his motives. Once I asked, "Why are you running?" and he answered, "I can't give you a concrete reason. It's something I feel I must do." That was reason enough for me. And in many ways I was relieved that the enigmatic period had come to a close. It had taken three strenuous years to build up to the ultimate day, during which George had not only carried out his duties in the Senate, but had kept up a lecturing tour so intense that it had gradually assumed the characteristics of an indefatigable, unending campaign; and he had also been weighted with responsibility as chairman of the Democratic Reform Commission, a job he took both out of a sense of duty and because, as he told members, "I do not ever again want to see another convention like the one in 1968." So, on the evening of January 18, 1971, George announced on television in South Dakota that he was a candidate for President. ". . . The kind of campaign I intend to run will rest on candor and reason; it will be rooted not in the manipulation of our fears and divisions, but in a national dialogue based on mutual respect and common hope . . ."

Some people, in fact many, thought George was foolish to announce so many months before the election — a full year earlier than any candidate in American history, save Andrew Jackson. But the small center of his support had begun to widen. Now it included a group of dynamic young workers, a growing number of more senior political advisers, dozens of campus organizers with unflagging spirit, networks of housewives who were believers, and a wide assortment of friends and workers, far too numerous to categorize or mention by name. They had faith in George, as did legions of other grassroots people suddenly willing to help financially. "Nobody's ever done this before," George had written to them in more than 200,000 long personal letters, timed to arrive on the day he announced his candidacy. "I want to run a campaign financed by tens of thousands of small campaign contributions. That's how I want to build my organizational base, not on a few big contributors." By the time $250,000 arrived in the mail George told me that he felt his instincts were right. I was not quite so sure.

On the day George paid the $500 fee and filed his papers for the primary race in New Hampshire, we flew up to Concord in a small private plane piloted by Len Greene, a New York businessman and one of George's earliest supporters. While we were circling in the traffic pattern to land, George reached over and tapped me on the knee. "Well, Eleanor, do you think you want to go through with this?" he asked. "That is like asking a woman in labor on the way to the hospital if she really wants to go through with it," I answered.

When I started to campaign alone in the primary elections for George, there were no planned decisions about doing this or doing that in a certain style. I slipped into my role as naturally as I slip into my clothes. I had learned back in the 1962 Senate race in South Dakota how much I enjoyed meeting people. I liked the personal contact — to me shaking hands is a very expressive means of communication, a transfer-ring of strength and support, not at all an empty ges-ture. I think I know hands; I feel through them; handclasps tell me a great deal. Being with voters on a one-to-one basis was the way I could help most.

The only calculated plan was for me to precede George into the states where primaries were to be held and where a McGovern presence could add to the nu-cleus of support that was already there. That became a pattern: initially, informal campaigning was con-ducted by me; then, as each primary election day drew near, George arrived and I moved ahead. Hopefully, when I got there, I rallied enthusiasm and defused the tensions of McGovern workers who were trying to de-

velop state-wide organizations without the backing of
regular party Democrats more inclined to support
other candidates.

In the beginning it was exciting. A friend from Chicago, Barbara Howarth, was my one-member staff and
traveled with me. We were aided by superbly moti-
vated, able young politicans in the field such as Gene
Pokorney and Joe Grandmaison, whose briefings about
local politics were concise but encyclopedic in scope. I
wanted to know everything. What did people do in
the towns I was going to visit? What were the issues
that concerned them? What about the history of the
region? What were they saying about George in New
Hampshire, Florida, Wisconsin, Massachusetts, Ohio,
California? There were twenty-three primaries; of
these George won victories in ten carefully selected
states where he concentrated his efforts.

Those early state elections were warm, cooperative
endeavors. In New Hampshire and Wisconsin, for example, I learned to expect cheery faces, pink from sub-
zero weather; blazing fireplaces and big bowls of homemade soup; narrow storefront headquarters with
George's picture in the window, banked by great snow-
drifts across which I had to leap; children as young as
six and seven helping with the mail; housewives filling
up bins with painstakingly handwritten appeals for
George and canvassing from door to door late into the
night; and financial backers, professional football
players, and movie stars — Henry Kimelman, Morris
Dees, Shirley MacLaine, Warren Beatty, Dennis

Weaver, Stewart Mott — showing up here and there in the middle of small crowds of shoppers and store-keepers, reviewing George's strengths. How inspired we were! Often I think about the young woman in a McGovern storefront headquarters who came up to me and said, "I'm one of those dedicated, hard-working, sacrificing people you just thanked for working for the Senator. Mrs. McGovern, I am not doing it for him. I am doing it for me." That is the way we all felt.

"Since I am completely free to say what I wish," I explained to people who asked if it made me nervous to be on my own, "George is taking his chances." Actually, the only time I know for sure that I embarrassed him was in New Hampshire. It happened during a guided tour of the radically right-wing Manchester *Union Leader*. A scheduled interview had been canceled after I arrived — thus the tour. I saw the whole plant, and then, in a ceremony performed with near reverence, my guide opened a door and allowed me to peek into the spare, beautifully paneled office of William Loeb, the editor and publisher. I was not quite sure what to say about the empty room, so I remarked on the portrait hanging over the desk. "William McKinley, isn't it?" I asked. "That is Daniel Webster!" I was told with marked disdain. Two days later, in an editorial signed by Loeb and prominently displayed on the front page of the Manchester *Union Leader,* New Hampshire voters were advised in dramatic terms that "if Mrs. McGovern is this ignorant of New Hampshire's favorite son, Daniel Webster, then

Mr. McGovern can go and peddle his wares else-
where." Anyway, I'm not sure that either McKinley or
Webster would feel at home in William Loeb's office.

In those days the polls showed that only 3 per cent
of the American voters supported George, and we told
each other that it seemed as though we were meeting
all of them personally. I was always behind schedule
and George was criticized sharply because he took so
much time to talk to individuals. "His decency as a
human being, let it be confessed, is a distinct liability,"
The Nation magazine reported, reflecting widespread
press reports that he was too low-key, a one-issue candidate, too unemotional, without charisma — but a
very nice person. More perceptive reporters saw his
real strengths. "George McGovern comes at you like
one of those big Irish heavyweights in the 1930's, a
little slow, but with the chin shut hard against the
chest, the jaw breaching out, coming on, daring you to
do your best," was Pete Hamill's description. "Like Jim
Braddock, he might be beaten, but you will know he
was there, he will not fold up on you, he will surrender
no dignity, and you will come away speaking about him
with respect. Sometimes, he will even win."

It did not take as long as I expected for the winning
to start. And with each victory the seriousness of our
purpose became a heavier load to bear.

From the first day I took off on a solo campaign,
until the general election was over, I (and every person
on my little staff) had trouble working out with Wash-

ington headquarters an appropriate, reasonable, meaningful schedule. Perhaps I wanted too much. There
is no question that I was a Presidential candidate's wife
who was caught between eras, and the subtle discrimi-
nation I felt was a severe introduction to male chauvin-
ism in politics. It was especially frustrating because
George had always treated my political intuition with
respect. During these days I hardly ever had a chance
to talk to him about my role — at least with specific-
ity — yet he knew I was struggling to define it, and I
knew that he knew. About halfway through the campaign it was reported back to me that he had said to
Gary Hart, "You keep telling me Eleanor is a potent
secret weapon. I think it is about time to start treating
her like one." But resources were limited and there
was little time to develop a completely separate campaign for me. Still, I had a tinge of resentment and
sensed that what was happening to me was inextricably
a part of a still murky area at the edges of the feminist
movement. For many — those whose job it was to figure out how to use me most effectively — I was not
Eleanor McGovern; I was George McGovern's wife.
For others — grassroots workers, supporters, voters —
I was the closest they would get to a national figure.
For some women I was betraying my very womanhood
by working on behalf of a man; for others I was evidence that caring about home and family need not
preclude caring about community and country.

My motives, I admit, were manifold — to take as well
as to give, to learn as well as to inform. I wanted

something for myself other than good press coverage; I wanted to learn about the United States firsthand. I wanted to cooperate and fit into the over-all election strategy; yet I was simply unwilling to don a scuba diving outfit or bathing suit or snowshoes or stand on my head in a yoga position (which Jane Muskie also refused to do) or put myself in the hands of an advance man who sometimes had less knowledge of people and local concerns than I had. I did permit myself, on dark, cold evenings, to be scheduled to stand in the snow outside of plant gates so that I could shake hands with the midnight shift of workers, most of whom either did not see me or ignored me in their rush to get home. In hindsight I would argue persuasively against the political value of such activities. And I did get caught by the cameras in a foundation-garment factory full of enthusiastic union supporters who presented me with an embarrassingly mountainous red-white-and-blue bra, after which I was reported to have said it had been "a very uplifting experience." And there is a picture of me standing somewhere on Wilshire Boulevard in Los Angeles with peace doves perched on my *head* that were supposed to have flown away into the sky, to symbolize the friendship of Asian-Americans for McGovern. There was also a time when I was campaigning with George and he impulsively reached down, picked me up, and held me high enough for a crowd to see, though I refused to cooperate when the television cameramen, who had missed the shot, cried, "Do it again!"

For the most part I resisted — or at least I tried to — empty gimmicky or unrealistic schedules pulled together at headquarters too often by men — yes, I will have to say that — whose perceptions of a political wife were either chauvinistic or out of date. It was a chronic pain to convince the decision makers that I was not interested in going along with George as "excess baggage," as Abigail McCarthy once described a candidate's wife, nor did I expect to be programmed into the kind of high-powered leadership role necessary for the candidate; nor was I interested in attending a string of functions pieced together solely for women. I looked for something in between, I suppose, designed just for me. I had a passionate belief in the need for change and in my ability to help George. I needed to affirm my years as a person nurtured in a political climate. And I had confidence in myself, in my insights and instincts, and I wanted others to have confidence in me too. In fact, it always came as a surprise when they did not. I remember that on the day Governor George Wallace was shot, George was out of town and I happened to be home; without giving it a second thought, I asked my next-door neighbor, Margot Hahn, to drive with me to the hospital to let Cornelia Wallace know I wished to help if I could. It was an impulsive gesture, and I expect that Mrs. Wallace would have done the same thing for me. That evening I had a call from headquarters. There had been a meeting of campaign officials, I was told, to discuss whether or not they were going to send me to the hospital. "I've already been there," I said.

In all fairness, I will concede, I struck one bargain with the schedulers that was honored throughout the primaries. It was purely self-indulgent and probably reinforced the image of a candidate's wife that many people seem to have. I insisted on visiting at least one day-care center or early-childhood-development project or experimental school on each trip. If I was going to campaign to be a "White House child advocate," I needed to know what was happening across the country. When I asked my friend Dr. Maria Piers, dean of Chicago's Ericson Institute, what to look for when I visited children's projects, she said, "Look at the children's faces. You will know right away if they are in a stimulating environment." And she was right. When young children clustered around me, begged to sit on my lap, kissed me, or asked me to take them home with me, they were not happy children. (In 1973 when I visited Anna Freud's day-care center in London, I was virtually ignored by the little ones.) I saw too many unhappy children in 1972 in schools, church basements, community centers; in grubby little painting smocks, on space-age jungle gyms, in anterooms spilling over with boots and mittens; children who told me, "I have to have my breakfast here," or "My sister's got something the matter with her," or "My mom and dad blew it." Of course, I saw happy children too, and they helped to make the campaign days shorter for me, though often it was suggested pointedly that there was minimal political value in spending so much time with them. That made no difference to me. More than once I refused to walk up and down a school hall and merely stick my head in the doors so that I could get back on schedule faster.

At no time was the ambiguity of my role as a candidate's wife more apparent than when I was called upon to stand in for George. I was reluctant to do so — but there was no one else — and it was excruciatingly difficult for me, especially to substitute at enormous Jefferson-Jackson Day dinners in big cities such as San Francisco and Baltimore, where I was usually seated above thousands of Democrats on the dais with Ed Muskie, Hubert Humphrey, Scoop Jackson, and other potential candidates. I agonized unreasonably over the preparation for those appearances because I felt so responsible for the impression I was making on George's behalf. In fact, I was once aghast when George was late in arriving at a huge Milwaukee rally, attended by all the potential candidates and a large representation of the national media, and Governor Pat Lucey advised me that I would have to say something off-the-cuff about George. That evening I was seated at a table for candidates' wives next to my old friend Mary Hoyt. I had recommended her as a press secretary for Jane Muskie in the 1968 Vice-Presidential race and I knew she had just resigned as Washington editor of the *Ladies' Home Journal* to travel with Jane once again. Nevertheless, I clutched her arm and whispered desperately, "I don't even have a piece of paper and I am going to have to give a speech." So she fished a notepad and pencil out of her purse and I started scribbling furiously. A few minutes later

George strode into the auditorium. "I think I'm almost sorry he made it," I confessed to Mary. "I have a great spontaneous speech here about him."

It was not at all unusual for George and me to see each other briefly in crowds of hundreds, then go our separate ways. We talked a great deal by phone. His aides sometimes complained that he would disappear at crucial moments and they would find him in a phone booth talking to me, or searching through a newspaper to see if anything had been printed about my little campaign. One weekend, when I went home, I found a letter he had left on my dressing table for me. "Dearest Eleanor," he wrote, "I have been reading the wonderful things you have told the press about me in your travels. Needless to say, I treasure your kind words. But do not jeopardize either your credibility or mine by making me sound too good. I have, as you know, a generous measure of faults, weaknesses, and errors. As De Gaulle once said: 'Every man of action has a strong dose of egotism, pride, hardness, and cunning. But all those things will be forgiven him, indeed, they will be regarded as high qualities, if he can make them the means to achieve great ends.' I confess to all the faults De Gaulle describes and more. I only hope they can be turned to worthwhile ends. Love, George."

During the spring of 1972 about the only time our family was together as a unit was on a primary election day. Ann's husband, Wilbur, was still in South Dakota in college and Ann had moved into our Washington house to be a surrogate mother for Mary Kay and Steve, while I campaigned for four days each week, then tried to be at home at least for three. Teresa was either away or campaigning with her dad. And Sue and Jim now were parents of our second grandson, Matthew. (I took a week off when he was born for what I called my "baby week" in spite of an irate staff member who complained that "the kid will be around for a long time.") I missed home. But when I was there, I felt as uneasy as when I was away, and I found it increasingly difficult to know where I was needed most. The comfortable times were when the family gathered at some hotel in some primary state in a solid McGovern front for those tension-filled election nights.

The children say now that they were always sure that George was going to win in Wisconsin. I was not at all certain. I remember that as I walked into a smoky Milwaukee hotel room filled with top staff people, Pat Cadell, our pollster, looked away from his pad and pencil and figures and said, "This is it!" Everyone wanted to hurry downstairs to the ballroom to join the victory celebration, our first. "Let's not be in such a rush," I kept saying to George and the family and the staff. "Let's wait until we are absolutely sure of this." There was never a primary election night when I did not have similar pangs of concern.

"Something's up when the society editor of the Superior *Evening Telegram* is more interested in hashish than hairdos, when a candidate's wife is readier to discuss Phase Two than foie gras. What's up, apparently, is that women voters are no longer happy hearing only about home and hearth, even from a candidate's wife; they want to hear about the issues," wrote John Pierson of the *Wall Street Journal,* after taking a three-day campaign trip with me. Pierson's story pointed out that only three people had asked Jane Muskie what her husband liked to eat, and that she and Muriel and Mary Lindsay and Martha Hartke were campaigning, as I was, alone. The title of the piece was, "Wives of the Candidates Take to the Hustings to Help Their Spouses; Issues like War, Unemployment, Occupy Eleanor McGovern on a Hectic Wisconsin Trip." I liked that publicity better than the Washington *Star-News* headline over pictures of Muriel and me, "Still friends, though locked in combat." It was humiliating to be compared to old friends, to be asked to appear on television debates together, to be put into the position where one woman inevitably had to upstage the other. Every time I saw one of the other wives, I was filled half with empathy and half with anger at the awkward position we were in.

Each of us had different campaign styles, colored by our personalities, our pasts, our husbands, our families, our experiences, our interests, our talents. Muriel's way of campaigning was to hand out cards that had her recipe for the hearty beef soup that "sustains Hubert Humphrey's vim, vigor, and vitality" on one side and an autographed color picture of her on

the other. She had found her stride after years on the
hustings in Minnesota and after assuming heavier responsibility as a Vice President's wife. Jane Muskie
seemed right at home in the larger, more traditional
women's brunches, luncheons, and teas, and was talking freely about the issues. She had learned to expand
and refine her Maine-style campaign skills in the national campaign in 1968. We were very different types
of women but were stuck with the same label: "The
candidate's wife," locked into "little women" politics —
"What's he like? What does he do?" At the same time
we were expected to be highly opinionated and sharply
aware of our husband's positions on all the issues.
During that spring I was fielding questions in living
rooms, meeting halls, and at press conferences about
Vietnam, the Middle East, China, wage-price controls,
welfare, social security, and drugs, and trying desperately to interpret George's fifty-four-page alternate defense budget. One night I told him how hard it was
for me to explain. "I wish someone would ask *me*," he
said wistfully. "The press more often asks me some superficial questions about endorsements or staff squabbles." Difficult as it was, I liked the challenge of explaining George's viewpoint, and now and then I felt I
had converted skeptics. Once, for instance, I saw a
young man in a huge crowd in San Antonio holding up
a poster depicting George saying, "Isolation Now, Isolation Tomorrow, Isolation Forever." I marched up
and asked where he had found the poster. "I made it
myself," he announced. "Well, it's inaccurate," I said

firmly. "McGovern wants to cut defense waste." After I took down his name and address and promised to send him literature, I told him who I was. "Wow!" the boy said. "That is unbelievable. That's enough to make me vote for McGovern." I have often wondered if he did. A candidate's wife *never* really knows whether or not she is effective.

New Hampshire, second; Florida, sixth; Illinois, second; Wisconsin, first; Pennsylvania, third; Massachusetts, first; Ohio, second; Nebraska, first; Maryland, second; Oregon, first; Rhode Island, New Mexico, New York, first, first, first, first, first — the election results somehow linked together, gradually related to one another, then to a clearer political picture, like a puzzle picture that takes shape as lines are drawn from one numbered dot to another.

Some primaries were more special than others. Massachusetts was an exhilarating victory, after which we drove to the airport to send off to the next primary states what Paula Locker (a former president of the Women's National Democratic Club, who had replaced Barbara Howarth as my staff person) described as the "scruffiest-looking army of beautiful, dedicated kids I have ever seen." That night Kathleen Kennedy showed up at the airport too, and gave George a book of quotes treasured by her father. And Teresa cried because we never had time to stop and savor winning.

California was a big, important victory that surged to a climax amid currents of conflicting emotions: incredulity and regret over Hubert's uncharacteristic attacks on George's positions; joy and relief when Ann's second son, Kevin Mead, finally triumphed in his twelve-hour struggle to enter the world on election day; and exhaustion building up, aggravated by the unreal sense of displacement that comes in a campaign.

New Jersey is fixed in my mind because, by then, I was like the little engine that kept saying, "I think I can, I think I can," though I was not entirely sure that I could make it all the way uphill. I was drained; yet my schedule called for two more day-care centers, a luncheon, handshaking in Klein's department store, a headquarters opening, and three fund raisers at night, after which there was a fifty-mile drive to New York. Then a significant thing happened: on the last stop, late at night, when I literally crawled out of the car and stumbled into an auditorium full of Democrats, I was met with tumultuous applause, foot stomping, hand clapping, and roars of approval, so life-giving, so energizing, that I knew I was having my first taste of the ravishing way campaigning politicians are seduced, revived, and kept going by friendship and flattery.

Chapter X

The Longest Summer

On Saturday, July 8, when our huge jet roared down the runway and lifed southward toward Miami in the pale July sky, I could not help thinking back on our relatively brief and uncomplicated trip to the Democratic Convention in Chicago four years before. This time, however, there were fifteen family members, forty-three staff, twenty-two delegates, many friends, a large and impressive sampling of the national press — and everything at stake. It was no longer George's mission, his campaign. Millions were now involved, good people who counted on George to end the war, to do something about the disastrous state of the economy, to insist on government they could respect. A growing sense of responsibility to them had for weeks dropped a light cloak of soberness over any merriment we felt. Neither George nor I was expectant that afternoon; rather, we told each other we were determined not to look ahead or behind, but to meet each moment as it came. In retrospect I remember so few details of the Miami Convention — in spite of its importance in our lives — that I am forced to conclude that my anxiety level must have been very high. In fact, about all I can say for certain is that July 1972 was for me the beginning of the longest summer in my life, when in the course of events we were swept up and over the crest of the wave onto a desolate beach.

Not long ago Sue and I were reminiscing about Miami, and she said: "By the time we got to the Doral Hotel, I had become conscious of always being *above* the rest of the world *physically*. If we were not in an airplane, looking down, then we were on the top floor of a hotel, looking down, and this reinforced my sense of isolation, unreality, of 'being at the top.' Nobody is prepared for that feeling." She is right. I remember longing for what was familiar. Perhaps that is why I drew so heavily on family that week. The whole family had grown accustomed to hotel "presidential suites" during primary elections, but none of us felt quite comfortable secluded in the castlelike elegance of the Doral penthouse suite, with its tangerine ceiling, its ornate wallpaper, the brocade furniture, and sheer gold curtains softening an endless view of the Miami skyline. Nothing could erase the fact that we were up there, set apart from the larger operation in the command post and the "boiler room" of delegate-counting political operatives and in 260 other fancy rooms, filled with what Gary Hart described as "an absolute zoo" of "meetings, egos, confusion, and crises." Although we were the center of the operation, we somehow felt outside of it. I took some comfort in knowing that, no matter what happened, at least we were together.

By that time I had grown impatient with being pushed. There is something in my nature — astrology lovers say it is a Sagittarian trait — that balks at being told what to do. I have always coped quite independently, which is not at all possible in a team effort as labyrinthian as a Presidential campaign. I knew that. But by the time I arrived in Miami, I felt caged. Reportedly there were 3019 delegates and 15,000 media persons, and although I had a sense of responsibility for making a good impression on them, I needed also to slow down and find my natural pace again. I was like a washed-out photo, overinterviewed and overexposed. In the previous weeks, as it had become increasingly apparent that George was headed for the nomination, I had been discovered by the national press, and this new aspect of campaigning had made me so tense that I had asked Mary Hoyt to be my press secretary again. Now I had a small staff: Paula, Mary, and Sue Vogelsinger, a long-time, loyal volunteer, who worked in the White House during the Kennedy years and was helping to keep my appointment book. I had suggested strongly that they leave some blank spaces on my Miami schedule for rest and family — and all of my evenings free. Although I knew George could not be with me, I wanted to be in the middle of the action at Convention Hall.

We had a marvelous plan, sensible and adjust-able — a few interviews, a few events, and lots of time for me. Yet the very next day I was hopelessly late in meeting a group of press correspondents because I was in the penthouse pullman kitchen washing the dishes after cooking bacon and eggs for George and the children and the grandsons and the other relatives and staff who wandered in and out. "I can't tell the press that you're late to talk about being a potential First Lady because you're scrubbing a frying pan," Mary said impatiently. "Then go out and find me a cook," I answered. That night I had help in the kitchen. Paula and Sue had found Libby Strauss for us — a cheerful, unflappable gourmet genius, office coordinator of the Florida headquarters, whose political strategy during the primaries had been to feed volunteers so well that they never left the office for meals. Libby had dug into her freezer and brought up to the suite crêpes stuffed with turkey and Mornay sauce, chocolate cups filled with ice cream, individual fruitcakes, butter cook-ies, butterscotch squares, and homemade bread; and from her refrigerator, cheeses and blueberries and bagels; and from her pantry a set of her favorite pots and pans. Libby made us feel human. She cooked old-fashioned pot roast for George, by now absolutely repelled by hotel food; and heavenly homemade choc-olate mousse, which the family dipped into all day. She kept everybody else out of the suite while the family ate meals together; she answered the telephones. She even argued with George when he told her that he thought the country was ready for a Jewish Vice President. (He was thinking of Senator Abe Ribicoff, whom he had long liked and admired.) Libby stayed with us throughout the summer and fall, traveling with the campaign now and then, taking over the house in Washington at other times. I came to call her a "co-mom." She said others called her "Senator McGovern's Jewish mother." She was all of those things, and much more. She helped feed both our bodies and our souls in Miami.

When I review my schedule of the daytime hours at the Miami Convention, I dredge up memories of triviality counterposed with matters of consequence. For the first time, and I hope the last, I was asked at a press conference by Sally Quinn about the type of lingerie I wear; then later on the same day was placed at the same table with Muriel Humphrey at a fashion-show luncheon, picketed by women delegates passing out leaflets that read, "The problem is not what you wear at the convention; the problem is what you do." I can recall clearly Mary Kay's birthday, when she seemed to feel the necessity to repeat to each member of the family, "I am seventeen today, I am seventeen today," which at the time seemed less pressing than how we were going to arrange pictures of the family together, pictures of Ila and me together, pictures of George with delegates, relatives, supporters, and fund raisers.

And I won't forget easily the abrupt change in my mood after the hilarious entertainment at a luncheon honoring women candidates and incumbent Congresswomen, when I walked out to discover that a detail of Secret Service agents had been indefinitely assigned to me because there had been an especially disturbing threat on George's life. (He had experienced several such threats, but never mentioned them to me until months after the campaign was over).

When I first saw the delegates at Convention Hall, I had a great urge to throw back my head and laugh with joy. A lot of people have told me that the television image of the Miami Convention was disastrous because of the way people looked. But I appreciated what I saw as an accurate portrait of the grassroots America I had come to know in state after state. In Bob Greene's diary, *Running,* he described his reaction to delegates on a shuttle bus ride from the Hall to the hotel: "All these months everyone had been reading about the impact of the McGovern party reform commission and how it has diversified the party, but it didn't really register with me until tonight. I figured I would get to the convention and see a hall full of gray politicians, with a token woman here, and a token black there, and a token kid over there. But that's not how it is at all. The people on the bus made me grin. It's as if a television producer had decided to include every imaginable group in a fantasized version of what a crazy political convention would look like. The bus

had college kids, old black women, construction super-
intendents, bankers, and a woman in a gorgeous slinky
black dress and a canvas army bag."

In contrast to the 1968 convention proceedings,
when I felt oddly disconnected from events, this time I
was acutely aware of my feeling of esteem for George
and my respect for the many hard-working people who
had made it possible to go so far; love and sentiment
was strong, always just beneath the surface.

We had two family boxes, but one was across the
Hall from the other, and neither had enough seats for
the whole family, which meant hurt feelings for some
member every night. (Although it was said that the
McGovern forces "controlled" the convention, we certainly did not. One of the saddest moments of the entire campaign was when I heard that Ila had been
turned away from Convention Hall without a place to
be seated on the night that George was nominated.) I
was not surprised, but I was dismayed, to find Muriel
in the Humphrey family box a few feet away. There
we were again! I knew that the outcome of the vote to
uphold Hubert's refusal to turn over his California delegates to George was every bit as important to her as it
was to me. George needed 1509 delegates to win the
nomination, and we did not have them without the
Californians, rightfully ours after the winner-take-all
primary, as had been agreed beforehand by each of
the candidates. George had publicly said that the Stop
McGovern effort was an "outright political steal," and
now the fruits of three years rested uneasily on the suc-

cess of our forces in steering a course through some delicate problems concerning a South Carolina challenge and into the safer waters of voting on the California matter. Even without the cliffhanging vote, emotions were sky-rocketing — with George Wallace's appearance on the podium in a wheelchair, with California legislator Willie Brown, crying "Give me back my delegation!", with the mixed signs of alarm, surprise, consternation, elation, smugness, and confusion on the faces of Gary Hart, Jean Westwood, Frank Mankiewicz, Pat Cadell, Rick Stearns, Jeff Smith, and other McGovern staff people on the floor, who came up to the box from time to time to explain what was happening behind the scenes.

After we won the important vote, Ann and I went backstage to the NBC television trailer for an interview with Ed Newman. We were gone about half an hour, and when we returned to our box, Muriel's nearby seat was empty. The next day, after Hubert and Ed Muskie dropped out of the race, the newspaper pointedly mentioned that Muriel had walked out of Convention Hall without speaking to me. I have always been sorry about that. I am sure Muriel knew, as I did, that it was a misinterpretation by a reporter unaware of the circumstances.

That night I did not want to leave Convention Hall. I wanted to stay with our people. I couldn't get enough of the good will that radiated toward me from McGovern delegates on the floor below the box. And it was three o'clock before I crept into the bedroom in the suite where George had fallen into a dead sleep. It seemed inane to wake him up and congratulate him, but that is what I did.

Dick Dougherty, George's press secretary, wrote in his book, *Goodbye, Mr. Christian,* what it was like for George when he was finally formally nominated two nights later. "He was sitting in his shirtsleeves off to the side of a large television set in the living room of his suite. He was holding a cigar in his long fingers and rolling it idly between them. The roar of the convention crowd filled the room. I saw no change of expression on McGovern's tired face as family and friends moved in to kiss him or shake hands. The absence of drama, of the electric shock of victory, was, as I say, natural. Yet it seemed somehow unjust. He had worked so hard for so long. He had been mocked and slighted. He had literally shaken American politics to its foundation. More was called for than handshakes and kisses. The earth ought to have trembled under Miami Beach. Comets should have shot across the sky."

As for me, when the time came for the roll call, when the final moment arrived for us to know how many delegates were pledged to George, I sat back in my box seat and pulled a tattered old blue notebook out of my evening purse and started to keep count. I still have it. Even when we went over the top, and pandemonium broke loose, I kept right on adding up the delegates, just to be sure.

In a way, it is regretful that the traditional scenario

for political conventions calls for a candidate at the time of his nomination to be apart from those who have stood up for him. It did not seem fair for me to be in the middle of the bedlam at Convention Hall, surrounded by our children, bathed in favor, drowning in roars of "We want McGovern! We want McGovern!" And when Henry Kimelman, one of our oldest friends and supporters, unexpectedly lifted me up and stood me on a chair so that I could see far across the floor of the Hall, I was not only fiercely embarrassed, but conscious that the moment belonged to George and that we were not sharing it together. That was when I asked Mary to borrow a phone to try to reach George for me, but she reported that he was talking to Hubert on one line and, on the other, Hyannisport had been placed on "hold."

The next day, during those well-publicized hours in which George's Vice-Presidential running mate was being picked, I went for a long, scenic boat ride with the children. I will never know why I left the hotel. Ordinarily I would have been eager to be nearby at such an important time. Quite obviously, it would have changed nothing if I had stayed at the Doral; different judgments would not have been made. Yet one downhearted night after the election George and I fantasized about what might have happened if we had been able to sit down together and quietly, privately, lengthily analyze, as we have done for so many years, some of the campaign's crucial decisions — such as the choice of a Vice-Presidential candidate.

It was reported that I was "openly, out-front opposed" when I walked into the suite and George told me that it was going to be a McGovern-Eagleton ticket. My memory is that I was merely surprised because I had never heard George mention the Missouri Senator as a possibility, and disappointed because I thought someone who had supported George in the primaries should be his running mate. It was not long before I picked up the phone and called Barbara Eagleton to say that Mary Hoyt was on her way over to see if she could help. I could remember distinctly how nerve-racking it had been when I had been unceremoniously dropped before the public eye. Besides, I was looking forward to sharing the spotlight with the blonde, attractive Barbara Eagleton, whom I had met and admired. My emanations were almost proprietary, and I could hardly wait for Mary to return to assure me that Barbara had wholeheartedly accepted events and was looking forward to the challenge as much as I was. Mary's report was that the scene in the Eagleton suite was already typically hectic. The Senator had been sitting by the television set in a beach robe, listening to a TV commentator talking about him; Barbara had been sitting on the couch, cool-looking in a pale aqua shift; the staff had been in and out with speech drafts, and the phone had not stopped ringing. According to Mary, Barbara Eagleton confided that she had a twin sister too, but that she did not see any need to talk to the press about such family matters. "That is going to be next to impossible," Mary warned. "You'd better get a press secretary and start figuring out how you want to handle personal things that you do not wish to discuss."

I had had a special dress made to wear in case George won the nomination, but I had never found time for a final fitting and I discovered it was much too small. So, on the night of George's acceptance speech, I put on a dress I had worn for several years and a treasured Indian squash-blossom necklace made of turquoise and silver. I had found the necklace in Los Alamos, New Mexico, on a primary-campaign trip when I had been forced, without warning, to speak to a group of atomic scientists — I talked about cutting back the military budget, even there at the nuclear-weapon research facility, though I had felt like an early Christian who had been thrown to the lions. Afterward I had bought the necklace in a little shop, rationalizing that I had been sent to do a job for which I was not prepared, and that I *deserved* the jewelry. "I *did* deserve it," I teased George as we sat in the Doral suite, waiting through the endless Vice-Presidential nominating speeches before we went to Convention Hall in the early hours of the morning.

It was a night of still-fresh wounds, but it was also a night of love. On the platform were many Democrats of stature whose dreams had been shattered — Ed Muskie, Scoop Jackson, Shirley Chisholm, and Hubert, who had fought so hard for the nomination of his party, who had dreamed of being behind the podium instead of George. I knew it was very hard for Hubert. "Defeat is hell," I wanted to say to my old, dear friend, with whom things would never be the same. I was seated next to him and I felt his presence keenly, but I could not find words. So I said nothing. George laid it out in his speech. Our personal anguishes were secondary; that was the important thing to remember. "Come home, America," he said, "from the killing of Asians to the healing of our own troubled land. From the loneliness of the aging poor, the despair of the homeless, the jobless, the uncared-for sick, to a society that cherishes the human spirit. From the bitterness of racism, to the dignity of brotherhood . . . to the land of your fathers, where we can rebuild our cities, revitalize our farms and towns, reclaim our rivers and streams. For what we need most of all is the assurance that we are part of a nation where we care about each other."

There is no spot in the world more beautiful to me than South Dakota's Black Hills. We have gone there on family vacations for years. It was a logical place to retreat after the convention, perfect for getting back in touch with ourselves.

My plans were firm. I was going to sleep late, take long hikes through the piny woods, and, when I had dispensed with the last national magazine interviews hanging over my head, sit under a tree and relax. I would have my family all around me. And Paula and Mary had come along to be there when the Eagletons came out so that we could coordinate plans with Barbara for the fall campaign. We would talk about the

campaign, I told them, but not until after, say, a trip to
Mount Rushmore, or a ride down to Rapid City to see
Aunt Blanche Frankforter, who likes to tell my friends
about the night of my birth when she held me over the
floor furnace to keep me alive, or a shopping expedi-
tion to Custer for leather and rare mineral-veined
rocks.

On the plane going out to South Dakota, Gary Hart
and Frank Mankiewicz told us all that they knew at the
time about Tom Eagleton's history of mental illness,
gleaned in bits and pieces, and characterized for them
by the Missouri Senator as occasional exhaustion, fatigue, melancholy. I can still remember the general,
dull foreboding that overcame me. Gary Hart has
written that he thought I asked immediately, "Will he
have to resign?" I do not remember that. But my lifelong interest in psychology had made me sensitive to
such words as "manic-depressive," "electric shock treatment," and "long-term hospitalization." Yet, by the
time we settled down in the mountains above Custer, I
was in a strange, languid state, at peace in our crude
but comfortable cabin with its huge old stone fireplace
that blazed at night when the air was cool; with Libby
in the kitchen creating delectable, mouth-watering sur-
prises; with my three little grandsons diverting me.
Sylvan Lake was glorious, cut-glass azure in the brilliant sun, surrounded by pungent pines forging up
through cracks in the boulders — beauty and tranquil-
lity, true reality, far removed from political problems.
I let immediacy slip away. I drank in stillness. "While

with an eye made quiet by the power of harmony, and the deep power of joy, we see into the life of things," Wordsworth wrote. That is what I longed for. I think now that if we had stayed in Washington that week, in the hurly-burly state that had become normal for us, we would have been pressed then to face up to George's serious trouble.

Let me say at the outset that no one person knows the whole story of what had come to be known as "the Eagleton Affair," not even George. He knows his part; that is all. I know mine, the part I shared with him; and that is all. The staff, the press, Tom and Barbara Eagleton — I suppose they all remember clearly certain actions and reactions, and perhaps more dimly other aspects of the drama. It will always be patchwork. Yet some of the facts have become lore I do not even recognize.

On the morning of July 25, less than a fortnight after the nomination, the Eagletons and George and I had a big, farm-type breakfast prepared by Libby at the round, lazy-Susan table in the corner of our living room in Cabin 10 at Sylvan Lake. After we finished eating, Libby left, and the four of us were alone. Tom Eagleton lighted a cigarette and elaborated on what we had heard, explaining that he had hospitalized himself on three occasions for "nervous exhaustion, fatigue, depression — whatever you want to call it," bouts that twice required electric shock treatment and psychiatric treatment. Once he had gone to Barnes Hospital in St. Louis for about four weeks, then to the Mayo

Clinic in Rochester, Minnesota, for a brief spell for a "nervous stomach," and again another time to the Mayo Clinic for several weeks. He said that his illnesses had stemmed from overwork, that he had not seen a psychiatrist except during the times mentioned, and that the only medication he took was an occasional sleeping pill. While he was talking, he lighted one cigarette after another, but Barbara sat very straight, poised, and quiet, and I said to myself, 'How calm and pretty she is!' Over a second cup of coffee we learned that before the Miami Convention, when Tom had been mentioned in the press as one interested in the Vice-Presidential nomination, the Eagletons had discussed at some length whether or not to keep the mental-health matter quiet if George should ask him to be his running mate. It had been a serious mistake to do so, both Eagletons conceded. In fact, Tom was very contrite and unequivocal about resigning from the ticket then or at any future date up to election day if controversy rose about his past. "I'll be off the ticket of my own accord," he told George. "You don't even have to mention it if trouble develops."

Our first reaction — and we have talked about it many times since — was deep-felt sorrow for the handsome, high-spirited young Senator, who had faced grave personal problems and had borne them in silence. And though we had expected trouble and it had turned out to be worse than we thought, we had not hardened our hearts or closed our minds. We wanted to hear the full story from Tom.

For most of the morning the four of us talked about the predicament, first alone, later with key members of George's and Tom's staffs. When George asked Barbara what she thought, she seemed surprised and said, "I don't know. I just don't know. I have no objectivity about this." I knew how she felt, and I was sympathetic when she told me that it had been difficult to handle friends who had wanted to write or send flowers to Tom when he had been in the Mayo Clinic undergoing electric shock treatments, because everyone had been told he was at Johns Hopkins Hospital for a minor stomach ailment.

Outside our cabin window, I could see the Secret Service agents standing like stick-figure sentries in the woods, facing downhill toward the road where a cluster of reporters and photographers waited for something to happen. Two able reporters from the Knight Newspapers, Bob Boyd and Clark Hoyt, whom George very much admired, knew the dimension of Tom's past illnesses and we knew they were going to print it soon; the others did not. By noon we all agreed that the facts should be disclosed frankly to the press, waiting at the lodge by the lake for their first crack at the two Democratic underdogs.

My heart was as pained as it had ever been when Tom Eagleton stood up publicly to tell his story. I was seated about three feet behind him and saw that he was perspiring through his jacket and trembling so hard that I feared he could not continue. I literally sat ready to break his fall. When the press conference was over, and the Eagletons came up to say good-by, he was still wiping the sweat off his face — but he was smiling. "Whew, I feel better!" he said. "I've been carrying that load around for twelve years!" Mary told me later that one of the Senator's top staff aides had said the same thing to her.

That night Libby had a huge standing rib roast in the kitchen and we invited George's press secretary, Dick Dougherty, and a campaign strategist, Fred Dutton, along with Mary and Paula to come to the cabin for dinner. The children brought in logs and we all sat around a crackling fire, talking quietly at first, then warming up to a joke here, a remark there, finally roaring with laughter at practically everything said. At one point, I remember, George showed Mary and Paula the cuff links of Black Hills gold his staff had given him for his fiftieth birthday, engraved "Come Home, America," and he told them, "Eleanor would have preferred the simpler message, 'Come Home!' " We thought that was excruciatingly funny. As the fire burned down, our hilarity grew, and sometimes we laughed so hard that we were nearly crying. In retrospect, I know, we were weeping behind our laughter. Our bizarre behavior, I am sure, was the only way to bear Tom's burden of twelve years that had suddenly been passed onto our shoulders.

The phone calls and letters started at once, most of them in opposition to George's statement that he was standing one thousand per cent behind Tom (an impulsive statement made in a compassionate moment), and the money for the campaign dried up overnight, and the staff was blistered by the press for sloppy work in choosing Tom for consideration in the first place. It seems to me that whether or not our staff asked Tom the right questions about his past, whether or not he was thoroughly "investigated," is irrelevant. A Senator does not conduct an FBI check on a colleague. It would be an insult. Every politician knows what his credits and debits are, and there is a tacit understanding that the facts go on the table. And one does not go out and look for trouble when a respected member of the Senate has been praised highly by such men as the Senators Gaylord Nelson, Walter Mondale, and Ted Kennedy, who recommended Eagleton to George as an ideal choice — they had had no inkling about his recurring emotional disturbances.

Our own family was divided on the question — at least, until the full story emerged. I think it was like that in many homes. One man told us not long ago, "I knew you were in trouble when I saw what happened in my own family. In the beginning I thought Eagleton should step down and later I thought he should not. My wife, on the contrary, thought he should not step down, but later decided he should. I remember thinking that if what was happening in my own family was representative of the country, you were in a real mess — it was a 'no-win' situation."

It was indeed. Hour by hour, unrelated events welded together to create a monstrous impasse: Jack Anderson's accusations of multiple counts against Tom for drunk driving; then word that Tom had switched to the offensive and would not step down voluntarily, perhaps not even if he was asked; increasingly, the harsh, uncompromising criticism of George for reconsidering his supportive stand; and, finally, the long, confidential hours on the telephone with doctors and psychiatrists, who were cautious but deeply troubled about the possibility that history might one day thrust a person with recurrent manic-depressive tendencies — some said the illness had a built-in periodicity — into the Presidency.

I have never felt more helpless in my life. There was nothing I could do or say to help George as we carried out the routine of a vacation that had assumed the overtones of a Greek tragedy. George played tennis; he took Timmy out on the lake in a boat; and on Steve's twentieth birthday he himself tried to blow out the trick candles on the birthday cake, then persuaded Steve to get out his guitar, and the two of them sat under the old-fashioned lamp hanging over the table and softly sang, "This land is your land, this land is my land." At the urging of a local merchant we donned suede jackets and hats and rode a few blocks in a Custer parade, preceded and followed by powder-dyed horses — shocking pink, poison green, egg-yolk yellow — and jalopies filled with tail-coated clowns, in spite of the fact that we both feel foolish in parades and George has said that wearing unaccustomed headgear is an invasion of his "personhood." One afternoon the family, the staff, and the press were guests of our old friend Joe Floyd, who showed the film *The Candidate.* (George saw his first movie, *Aladdin and the Wonderful Lamp,* when he was seven and has been a movie buff ever since.) He chuckled at the caricature politicians on the screen, in spite of the irony of some impersonations, but on the ride back to the cabin, when the two of us were alone except for the two Secret Service agents in the front seat, he put his head back and closed his eyes for a long time. The he said, *"Oh, God!"*

The next day, when our plane left South Dakota and headed back toward Washington, I told one of the children that when a plane flies low enough across the prairies, you can still see the old wagon tracks. They are covered with grass now, and the grass is a different color, but the tracks are still there. That was the way it was for the campaign now. The joy was gone for us — and nothing would ever seem the same again.

Every adviser George consulted confirmed his ever-growing conviction that he had no option but to ask Tom to step down from the ticket. After several meetings the Senator agreed, although he made his resignation conditional on the release of a press statement he had drafted saying that health was not an issue.

In Timothy Crouse's book *The Boys on the Bus,* an exposition of press coverage of the 1972 campaign, he summed up the Eagleton resignation this way: "The newsmagazines served as Eagleton's best forum for self-beatification, but not his sole forum. The newspapers gave Eagleton loads of straight coverage, thus allowing him to play the victim and to establish mental health as a red herring issue. The real issue, as the *New York Times,* the Washington *Post,* and the Los Angeles *Times* pointed out in editorials, was the difficulty Eagleton had experienced in telling the truth. Eagleton's great victory over both McGovern and the press consisted in the agility with which he appropriated the hard news columns for his own designs — namely, to portray himself as a martyr for the cause of psychotherapy, a totally cured man who was wrongly suspected of being dangerously sick." Those words may sound harsh to some, especially when it is clear that Tom Eagleton is a bright, effective Senator with a promising future, who might be every bit as creative in politics as a Van Gogh was in art, an Ezra Pound in literature, a Wilhelm Reich in psychology, or many, many others. But in George's and my view it was not right for him to aspire to the position "a heartbeat away from the Presidency," that awesome, stressful, highest office, in view of his medical experiences. It is a judgment we will have to live with for the rest of our lives. Only history can test the credibility of all who were involved in what was for us the tragic summer of 1972.

Chapter XI

Winging It

For a candidate's wife a state primary election and a nationwide Presidential election are about as dissimilar as having a couple over for cards and sandwiches and having a formal five-course dinner for visiting royalty. To carry that analogy farther, the candidate's wife can be likened to a hostess who has been told she may hire a butler to serve an elegant dinner party, but that she will have to make do with her everyday dishes and nobody in the kitchen to help. She seldom has her own plane, her own group of managers and advisers, or a cadre of advance persons, speech writers, secretaries, baggage carriers, communications experts, and other workers to keep her campaign on the rails. Yet at times she may travel farther, give more speeches, shake more hands, and talk to more reporters than her husband.

Whether the efforts of a political wife are truly effective, whether she actually influences a voter's vote,
whether she can accurately portray her husband as a
human to the public, is open to question, and I believe,
though I am not sure, that Muriel Humphrey, Jane
Muskie, and other active campaigning wives would
agree. Pat Nixon has said, however, that she stays "divorced from the campaign issues which can make people feel uncomfortable, uninformed, or stupid," and I
respect her right to make that judgment. But in my
case I think I would have felt "uncomfortable, uninformed, and stupid" if I had stayed home in 1972. I
thought I could be a listening post for George, as well
as a source of information about him. I thought I
could shed some light on certain issues. I wanted to
meet blue-collar workers, discuss day care with ethnic
groups, inspire the apathetic, middle-aged voter, talk
to jobless youths, and find out what communities need
in order to help children. My aspirations were quite
unreasonable. A national campaign does not lend itself to a thoughtful, give-and-take pace. If I had the
1972 campaign to relive, I would do things differently.
As a candidate's wife, I would campaign less, and I
would campaign better. At least, I would not allow
myself to be swept into the maelstrom of national politics without having more to say about why and where I
was going and what my contribution could be.

After we left the Black Hills to start campaigning
again, George went one way, the children another, and

I traveled across the country, mostly on my own, until shortly before the election. Now and then McGovern paths would cross, or I would go on the "Dakota Queen II" for a few days. But our campaign strategy called for separate visits to major media markets by all of us and by George's ebullient new Vice-Presidential mate, chosen in a historic Democratic "mini-convention," Sargent Shriver and his wife, Eunice.

Traveling with me was a staff of two, Mary Hoyt and Margot Hahn, my next-door friend, who had never worked professionally but brought a note of levity to our group. Sue Vogelsinger stayed in Washington headquarters with a secretary, Lyn Bickel, to take over the thankless, pressure-prone task of hammering out my minute-by-minute schedules, all subject to revision, cancellation, augmentation, argumentation, and often bore little resemblance to what had been promised by overenthusiastic Democrats or what was realistically, logistically possible. And toward the end of the campaign, when I was sometimes in three states in one day with an indeterminate number of press, Didi Massey and Karly Wade, two bright young women, were assigned as "advance persons" to go ahead and smooth the way.

A Secret Service detail was assigned to me around the clock — usually one male agent and one female agent. (In 1972 Secret Service women were used for the first time.) As far as they were concerned, my name was "Redwood II," in keeping with George's code name, "Redwood I." My detail was always within range of call: when at home, in a trailer parked by the front door, which our Labrador, Atticus, appreciated because he loved to be with people in the house and out; when on the road, in a command post next to my hotel or motel room; when in motorcades, on the front seat of the car; and when on the public scene, if crowds threatened to swallow me up, or television cameras swung too near my head — I've had my share of black-and-blue marks — somehow Garrick or Skip or David or John or Laurie or Denise or Sue, whichever team was on duty, slipped near to form a comforting, protective shield. I do not think being a Secret Service agent is easy. All too often they are censured for firmness or for being conspicuous in photographs, but they have an exacting task and they are professionals. I well remember how pretty, blonde Denise coolly extricated herself from a potentially embarrassing situation by shaking her head when she found herself with me on an outdoor platform with Bronx politicians, members of the New York Knicks basketball team, and the singing "Temptations," and each of us was asked to stand, one by one, to be introduced.

I learned, although I did not want to know, that candidates' wives, like other public figures, are subject to occasional threats: "Don't go to Southern California"; "Eggs are going to be thrown at you on Labor Day." (We had never heard of "dirty tricks," but on Labor Day our plane was sent to the wrong airport, the sound system did not function, and a few days later, when a charter was mysteriously late, our schedule was ruined.) That was why it was neccessary for my agents to check out ladies' rooms, to "sweep" our hotel suites, to be sure that room-service trays were all right, or to be actively concerned when the schedulers suddenly diverted us from a commercial flight to a scary, little private plane in which we had to fold ourselves up with our luggage under our feet and cold, box-lunch chicken in our laps. Many times the Secret Service and airline representatives eased us through waiting lines and took care of tickets and baggage and luggage stubs, or brought me paper cups of coffee in inevitable "holding rooms" in the bowels of busy airports where I waited as a traveler with the pseudonym "E. Morgan." Nevertheless, I felt more comfortable when I was less privileged, and I liked it when a passenger or a stewardess would come up to chat or to tell me they were going to vote for George or to wish us well. My Secret Service agents became my friends. And now once in a while I run into them in Washington and we talk about the time I split off in a limousine from George's motorcade to campaign by myself — and his enormous entourage followed *us;* or about the hot day that Margot wandered off for a soft drink and was accidentally left behind, but ran so hard to catch up that she *passed* our motorcade, which she always called our "cortege."

In my mind's eye I see miles of macadam freeway, coiling between airports and city centers, and bushel baskets with sheaves of briefing papers from which I frantically tried to extract valuable kernels. No two stops were ever alike, so I was never sure if I would be handed a three-by-five card such as I received in Pennsylvania, saying, "Standing by the fence is so-and-so who has had the chicken pox since you were here in the primaries," or a twenty-one-page briefing dossier sprinkled with marginal comments, such as "She hates politics," or "In terms of organizational politics and savvy, he's old for his age." Attached to that last one were Xeroxed clippings of recent newspaper articles that had a bearing on the election, including quotes that were circled and marked, quite pointedly, "A good answer." I can still see Pepsi crates on which I had to climb up when microphones were too high, and I can hear complaining reporters who said my voice could not be heard over the crowd.

I remember how I worried about my memory. When Steve was asked how he would use unlimited power, he said that one gift he would give was "a computer for Mom to hold all of her information so she won't forget." My debating experience had helped to prepare me to think on my feet; still, I forgot things sometimes, or it would slip my mind where I was and why — was I soothing hurt feelings, helping to raise funds, or communicating to people who needed pepping up? It mattered to me. I wanted to talk directly to audiences whenever I could, to *reach* them. On one occasion, when I asked a person about a forthcoming event, I was told bluntly, "All you have to worry about is being nice to so-and-so, because he's *rich, rich, rich.*" That approach to politics, to people, appalled me.

Once in a while, on weekends, George and I would

be in Washington at the same time, and when possible, we would sneak through the back fence (the press was staked out across the street) and sit in the sun around the Hahns' swimming pool while George made political telephone calls. But usually Mary or Sue had set up appointments for me to be briefed, say, by Ted Van Dyke, who headed the issues division of the campaign, or to sit for the *Time* magazine cover, which I shared with Pat Nixon, or to film a TV feature covering one of my "normal" days. I longed to see old friends, and learned that in the chaos many had been inadvertently slighted. But there was simply not enough time and seldom enough patience. The *New York Times* food editor, for example, whose request to photograph me in the kitchen cooking George's favorite meal had been turned down, told Mary in disgust that he had not been treated with such negligence "since the days of Gaullist France." I am sure he did not realize that even when I was home, I had to unpack and repack my all-purpose, all-weather wardrobe, last pressed on a hotel bathroom floor with my traveling iron. Then usually one of the children with a problem to solve crowded into the bathroom while I shampooed, cut, and set my hair. Or Libby would come in to talk about the household budget or to help replenish the supply of vitamins, honey, wheat germ, high-protein cookies, and Nutrament that I carried in the bottom of my suitcase. I can remember many times talking to Mary on the telephone about the forthcoming schedule at the same time that I emptied on the bed my huge canvas McGovern shoulder bags, once described as "walking billboards," always stuffed with campaign buttons, Kleenex, mouth spray, felt pens, extra hose, and other things I might need if my bags got lost. And I learned to change my nail polish while Sue sorted through paper slips with names of people to thank for the toy Democratic donkeys, the hard hats, the keys to the city, the homemade pot holders, and other gifts Margot carried from stop to stop.

Sometimes, in the solitude of our bedroom, I would throw open the windows and try to make up for the times I had been too tired or too public to carry out my daily exercise regime. On the campaign Mary, Margot, and I had quickly started feeling unhealthy. Once when we were driving along in the back seat of a limousine, Mary invited us to join her in some relaxing facial yoga exercises — which she had started doing with such regularity between stops that Margot thought she had acquired a nervous facial tic — and we kept that up for a while, not caring how silly it may have looked to drivers passing by. And another time, when we were campaigning for a day with George, the three of us slipped away from an airport rally and did exercises on the floor of the "Dakota Queen II." But I think now that a deep gulp of fresh, pure air in the fall of 1972 might have knocked us right off our feet.

Even as the crowds grew larger, and each event more glamorous or highly publicized, inevitably, and usually without warning, something reminded me of George or of one of the children or of some individual who had touched my life. I remember how much fun it was to be on Dinah Shore's morning television show. I emptied out my pocketbook for her, revealed Ila's recipe of cottonseed meal, dried seaweed, dried blood, and wood ash for growing beautiful roses, and surprised myself by observing that Tensor reading lights had saved my marriage. Then pictures of the children and the grandchildren were flashed on the screen and Dinah sang "Try to Remember," and it was all I could do to remain composed. That day we flew directly from Los Angeles to New York for an evening benefit in Madison Square Garden for New York's Willowbrook mental institution, and right in the middle of an earsplitting rendition of rock music, I was overcome by memories of a young woman patient in a mental institution I had visited in the primaries who had looked up at me beseechingly and asked, "Am I always going to be like this?" One Friday in September there was a Washington press conference to announce an organization of women volunteers calling themselves "Friends of Eleanor McGovern," whose objective was to raise money in chain-letter fashion to help "keep Eleanor on the road." A last-minute change in my schedule had prevented the cochairmen, Anna Roosevelt Halsted, Eunice Shriver, and Sharon Percy Rockefeller, from being there, but the seventy-seven-year-old former Vice Chairman of the Democratic National Committee, India Edwards, flew in from California and the wives of many leading Democratic Senators and Congressmen showed up — including Barbara Eagleton.

When I leaf through the notebooks I carried in those

days, I find traces of sentiment, anger, elation. There are so many emotions with which to cope on a campaign: frustration from feeling unprepared; anger at the exhausting extra events cranked into a full schedule; but, through it all, a generous measure of exhilaration, love, achievement. Signs of all these are clear in my otherwise smudged notebook pages, filled with inky shorthand hieroglyphics. My notebooks were my security. When one filled up, I bought another. Often when I was scribbling, I overheard reporters asking Mary, "What's in there?" She would shrug and point out that I was prone to quote everything from the Sermon on the Mount to Desiderata, or that I needed military-defense statistics or facts about George's economic-conversion plan. Most important to me were key phrases that gave me a takeoff point for a speech, for those moments when I did not know what to do but was told, "Oh, you'll think of something to say," or "Guess you'll just have to wing it." Some important pages in the books showed these lines of thinking: "What is woman? Nothing but one of nature's agreeable blunders." "It is of little consequence what we know, what we think, what we say; the only true consequence lies in what we do!" "Arthur Bremer said, 'My future is small, my past an insult to any man.'" "The only thing radical about George McGovern is that he has made specific proposals and he is not rigid and immutable." "Politics affects every facet of our lives whether we like it or not." "Young children are the only source of our future adults." There are pages and pages of reasons why I wanted to be a "White House child advocate," and never enough time to talk about that in the national campaign.

My notebooks remind me that the 1972 campaign was for me a unique, extraordinary learning experience acquired in factories, prisons, day-care centers, senior-citizen homes, voter-registration offices, and in meetings with Democrats and Republicans, young and old. Their pages remind me too that as each day passed, I felt more remote from the real campaign. I was in touch with people, but I was slipping out of touch with George. And there was much I wanted to say to him about holding firm as a center of strength in the midst of what was turning out to be a disaster for him. When we spoke by phone, he always had a lift to his voice, no matter how bad the day had been, and I knew he would not give up in spite of devastating polls, insistent criticism about the Eagleton affair, and the obvious fact that he was not getting his message across. If he would not weaken, neither would I. But I was increasingly incensed by revelations about the opposition, which made it more and more frustrating to realize that George was not being heard. Moreover, I was getting tired and irritable and tense about my own lurching campaign, and particularly about commitments I had made to be on "Meet the Press," to go to Woonsocket for "Welcome Home, Eleanor" night, to speak at Madison Square Garden, where I would be introduced by Rose Kennedy to twenty thousand people. Sometimes I felt like a leaf

that was being blown from place to place by random
gusts of wind, rising one minute and falling the next,
never in sight of ground.

On October 1, a beautiful fall Sunday, George went
with me to the NBC TV studios in Washington where I
appeared on "Meet the Press"; apparently it was the
first time a candidate's wife had been on the show in its
twenty-five-year history. When I sat down next to
Lawrence Spivak, facing Bonnie Angelo of *Time* magazine, David Broder of the Washington *Post*, Ron Nessen of NBC, and Elizabeth Drew, a writer and television commentator, I was so nervous that I was nearly
sick. For the first time I felt sure that what I was doing
could not help having some impact on the campaign,
although it was far from certain whether my views
about my husband's candidacy would be a plus or a
minus factor as far as viewers were concerned. I am
sure there were many campaign strategists who held
their breaths that day. But Mary reported to me that
George proudly whispered to her, "She always does
well, once she gets over her stage fright."

I got over it very quickly. When both Ron Nessen
and David Broder asked me if I really believed that
George could be elected President, I said, "I do!" and
reminded them that he had overcome almost insur-
mountable odds in each South Dakota election to reach
the point where he was. And when Bonnie Angelo and
Elizabeth Drew inquired what insights I had gained on
the campaign, I felt quite at ease telling them that I

perceived a national aversion to the war and a sense of powerlessness in the average voter, who felt he had such little control over his life that he was cynical about politics. The half-hour passed all too swiftly — I discovered I had a lot I wished to say — and it ended with a question from Bonnie Angelo that I was particularly glad to be asked.

"Mrs. McGovern," she said. "Your performance here today bears out the comparison that has been made from time to time that you are very much an activist in the way of the previous Eleanor, Eleanor Roosevelt. How do you feel about those signs 'Let's put another Eleanor in the White House'? And in the same breath let me ask: Eleanor Roosevelt was a subject of great controversy and at some points a disadvantage to her husband; is it worth that risk being an activist First Lady?"

My answer was: "I sometimes think my name is a disadvantage because I hold her in great esteem, and I think there is only one Eleanor. She was a great trailblazer. I think of myself as a woman who is campaigning for a man in whom I believe, and I believe in the things that he believes in. I would be campaigning as strongly for him if he were not my husband. Maybe there is a risk involved, but since I have the freedom to speak, and my husband doesn't know what I am saying when I go about the country — he does not tell me what to say — he takes that risk."

I was glad George was in the studio to hear that answer. I will be eternally grateful that he had confidence in me, total confidence. One never knows whether a political wife who speaks out freely is actually helping her husband, but there is plenty of evidence that she can sometimes hurt him.

On October 4 I started on an eight-day swing across the United States that was to be my last big solo campaign, although I did not know it then. Nor was I quite sure when I started out that I was going to lay bare my feelings about the state of the country along the way. All I knew for certain was that I felt accountable for what I considered a serious lack of information about George, about the war, about Richard Nixon, and especially about Watergate, which was being accepted with more humor than alarm by all but 3 per cent of the country — according to polls, 52 per cent had not heard of it yet. I was furious about this apparent apathy. I might have suspected that the adrenalin surging from my deep anger would give me the energy to keep pushing on — but would eventually leave me as burned out as an ash.

By this time I was getting favorable coverage from the national press, even those who had discovered that it was more demanding traveling with me, hopping off and on planes and in and out of cars driven by volunteers unaccustomed to motorcades, than it was to travel on George's jet or in his press buses. It made me self-conscious to have them along as I gave forth, over and over, the same answers in local press conferences, TV interviews, talk shows, telephone interviews, or in question-and-answer periods. Some reporters believed that I was privy to all campaign strategy and involved in a never-ending conspiracy to send up political "trial balloons." I was asked *how* I served as George's chief adviser, and *whom* I wanted to see in George's cabinet! It was ridiculous, but flattering. The fact was that I was winging it all the way, and at no time was it more apparent than on that last trip.

At our first stop in Springfield, Illinois, for example, after giving a prepared speech to a nursing association and visiting Lincoln's Old Capitol, I skipped lunch so that I could say a few words to a huge gathering of rural electrification workers, largely because I remembered what our farm had been like before milking machines or electrified chicken coops, and how different farming became when the lights went on in South Dakota. The next day, in Little Rock on an unexpected tour of the state fair with Governor and Mrs. Bumpers, I talked again about farm problems, this time with some young people in a barn — on camera for Italian TV! In Dallas, in a department store converted into a community college, I departed from my speech about enhancing inner cities and rose to a confrontation with a Nixon heckler who refused to believe that George would or could bring the prisoners of war back unless we *won* the war. And later, in Hayward, California, at Chabot College, in observation of the anniversary four years earlier when Richard Nixon, then a Presidential candidate, had said, "Those who have had a chance for four years and could not produce peace do not deserve another chance," I called on Americans to "retrieve our souls from the tragedy in Southeast Asia," and digressed from my speech to tell about a time that nearly broke George's heart when he walked through a hospital in Vietnam, tragically filled with silent but terribly mangled children.

When I first started talking about Watergate, I did not "check it out" with anyone. I just felt it had to be done. In my briefcase I had been carrying the draft of a speech written by a good volunteer, Mary Lou Friedman, who often gave me suggestions that were incorporated into my remarks. Mary Lou had come up with a phrase that pleased me very much, and I decided that a night rally in Kentucky — one of those states where I was welcome but George was not — was a good place to use it. As it turned out, Louisville's Durrett High School, whose auditorium was packed to the rafters with two thousand friendly, cheering, whistling Democrats, was definitely the right setting for pointing out how Americans were being what Mary Lou called "duped and cheated." Later that night Frances Lewine of the Associated Press, who was traveling with me, filed a story that said I had delivered Kentuckians a "give 'em hell" attack on the Nixon Administration. That was a mild report.

"How could anyone feel other than duped and cheated," I asked in a voice so strong that I was later told it sounded like a roar coming from me, "when taxpayers are forced to pay nineteen million dollars in export subsidies for five big grain exporters? How could anyone feel other than duped and cheated when headlines link the Justice Department and Mexican bank accounts?" I continued ticking off the list. "When there are at least ten million dollars in a secret fund that Republican leaders in Washington refuse to make public . . . when Watergate offices of our Democratic Party are bugged and burglarized in the middle of the night — not a caper but a sacred infringement of our Bill of Rights and our Constitution . . . when there is little hope of an unfair tax structure being changed . . . when an immoral war and high unemployment continues?"

Each time I cried out the words "duped and cheated," the crowd yelled, "We want more!" "Finally," I concluded, pounding the lectern, "what I am saying is that things *are not right* in our government today!" When I had finished, the band struck up some patriotic songs and people began to crowd toward me from all corners of the cavernous auditorium. Until that time, I had had a nagging guilt that perhaps I had taken the tough approach toward the Nixon Administration as much for retribution as from my genuine alarm about the state of the country. But as I moved through the crowds toward the motorcade waiting at the front door, I knew I would not worry about that again, that I would keep speaking out about the crimes in Washington, not necessarily because it was politically expedient to do so, but because for me it had become obligatory, personally inescapable. I felt more important to the campaign from that night on.

A few nights later I renewed the attack at a $1-a-plate bean supper at the Blessed Sacrament Church in Seattle, Washington. "The papers today are shocking!" I said in extemporaneous remarks that grew quite heated. "The FBI reports stories of forged letters, stories of investigations that go back to 1971, leaking false items to the press, stories of investigators following members of Democratic candidates' families and assembling data on their personal lives. Can you *imagine* someone following the children of Senator Jackson, of Senator Muskie, of Senator Humphrey, or my own children? . . . Those of us who are open do not even understand this kind of human behavior. We are vulnerable, vulnerable because we don't think like that." As I spoke, I tried to convey my belief that the theft of personal expression is much more offensive than the theft of personal property. I was shaking with anger.

"I am thankful we did not think of spying on Tricia and Julie Nixon! I am glad we don't think of using people with such contempt. We cannot accept this in our country — we cannot get out of step with our own best instincts. *And I cannot believe we will!*"

On the plane headed back toward Washington Fran Lewine of Associated Press and Nan Robertson of the *New York Times* came up to my seat and sang a good-humored song they had composed for me. All I can remember is that it started, "Buckle down, Woonsocket, buckle down; you can win, Woonsocket, if you buckle down." I wondered how clearly my exhaustion

showed. Weariness had been crushing me down,
down, and I was beginning to worry about holding up
until the election. I had long since realized that it was
useless to worry about the concept or direction of my
campaign, about the constant friction between Mary
and Sue and the schedulers in Washington. I had long
since learned that it was destructive to dwell overlong
on the unfair or hurtful observations I read about
George. But I was full of despair, and knew I had
begun operating in a sort of limbo.

I was a physical wreck too. In the beginning I had
started each day with an enormous breakfast of bacon,
eggs, grilled tomato, toast, and milk; now I could not
eat at all and had lost so much weight that my clothes
were pinned together. In the beginning we laughed
about not getting enough fresh air and exercise and
about being too tired to think straight. Now it was
worrisome, not only for me but for Mary and Margot,
who often had to carry the conversation with local
Democrats when I was spent — they had found themselves in Texas talking about "Nuci Lugent" and "Good
old JBL." Our biological clocks had broken down
from passing through several time zones every day,
and we no longer had normal reactions to air turbulence, or screaming sirens, or even the disheartening
sight of puffy eyes, grimy sleeves, and wrinkled hose.
By noon it seemed like the middle of the night, not just
the beginning of a longer day that would find us overcome by queasy, bilious feelings from the odor of another plane or the sight of another plate of gravy-

covered hamburger or chicken. I well remember that most mornings my eyes felt scalded and my arms and legs were as stiff and ungiving as though I were an astronaut stalking over the moon. And most nights sleep was merely a thin veneer.

In this state, the day after we returned to Washington, late at night after I had given another speech at a Jefferson-Jackson Day dinner in Frederick, Maryland, Dr. Lawn Thompson put me in the hospital for a few days of rest.

Occasionally, when the contrails of a jet pierced the fleecy clouds drifting over the Kimelmans' sprawling, hillside house in the Virgin Islands, I would think about the campaign and about George. But for at least a couple of late October days, Mary, Margot, Charlotte Kimelman, and I rested in the sun. We had decided to take the brief vacation after my stay in the hospital and the subsequent trip to Woonsocket for "Welcome Home, Eleanor" night, an exhilarating experience that had nevertheless drained my meager reserves. Below the Kimelmans' broad stone terrace, fringed with rustling coconut palms, richly yellow-green with crotons, hibiscus, rubber trees, and scented with sweet jasmine, the sloping hills of Water Island rose out of a blue sea. All around was peace. Charlotte Kimelman is a quiet, effortless hostess, who had our evening meals served on the patio in candlelight and knew we were much too tired to chat. Gradually the sun warmed our bones, the knots loosened, even a few weak rays of hope surfaced in my mind. But with perspective came the realization that I had a speech to prepare if I was going to say something meaningful to twenty thousand people in Madison Square Garden.

The affair was to be called "Star-Spangled Women for McGovern-Shriver," and it was being planned by Shirley MacLaine. (A week later the evening turned out to be a success, largely due to the gracious appearance of Rose Kennedy, who praised George as "a very able and very dedicated man.") Shirley's idea was to draw on the talents of top women entertainers, and to use men only in supporting roles; she wanted a speech from me that would appeal to the women's vote, based on antiwar ideology. "Just something eloquent and beautiful," she told Mary flatly. Her expectations disturbed me, but at that time millions of unsolicited letters were pouring into campaign headquarters and I was sure I could find a source of inspiration within them. That is why I had a briefcase stuffed full of mail with me in the Virgin Islands.

One hot morning after we had dipped into the Kimelmans' pool, Mary and I started talking about the speech and I brought out the letters and passed them around for everybody to read. We read quietly for about an hour. I cannot describe how I felt then without saying that suddenly there was no doubt whatsoever that George was doing the right thing. Most of the letters were from people who had never written to a politician before or contributed to a political campaign. And all of their dreams were spelled out, in childish block letters, in the spidery scrawl of the aged; some were eloquent, others were crudely simple. A woman in Cincinnati wrote that she could no longer endure the disgrace of Vietnam: "Do these mothers care less about their children than I care about mine?" she asked rhetorically. And a man from Santa Rosa, California, sent a few dollars but wrote that even if George became President and stopped the war ". . . it is too late for us because my only brother was killed in Vietnam." A student who had seen George on a telecast wrote that afterward he felt his "first sense of nationalism." "At twenty-seven years of age," he wrote, "I am a product of the God-is-dead generation, the country-is-dead generation."

As far as I was concerned, what was in those letters was a clear affirmation that people were hungering for their lives to count for something. And I thought about going home to Woonsocket. That night I had said, "To be useful is what matters." Perhaps what I should have talked about was my belief that politics *is* usefulness, even though that notion is cynically questioned by many today.

When the night came for me to speak in Madison Square Garden, after all the entertainment was over, I elaborated on the theme that had taken hold in the Virgin Islands. "We have power," I implored a vast audience I could not see beyond the footlights. "We have power right here in our hands. We have power to change our world. And we must not feel helpless to act. We must not be intimidated by the faceless 'they'

we hear so much about — the 'they' that control our lives. For let me tell you what I now know about you — and about us. Let me tell you that this crucial campaign has taught me that *we are they!* We are the only ones who can make life worth living."
I believe that.

Almost exactly one year later, Mary and I sat on the Kimelmans' sunlit terrace in the Virgin Islands with Henry Kimelman, our loyal friend and earliest supporter, who was George's finance chairman. We were talking about the significance of the money that had fallen out of those letters in October 1972. It had been the first time in American politics that so many voters had helped to swell a campaign chest until it totaled more than thirty-two million dollars. They had contributed 80 per cent of our funds. We had not had any deals with vested-interest backers — the oil companies, the big banks, the who's who of American finance. We had had some large contributions from a few public-interest contributors, mostly young idealists with inherited wealth; and we had had some sizable contributions from "ego trippers," men who were seeking recognition. But most of our finances came in modest amounts from millions of average voters. In fact, in the closing weeks of the election there had been such a deluge of mail with one dollar, five dollars, ten dollars, and more, a backlog of so many thousands of pieces, that all of the paid staff and volunteers at headquarters, including Henry, Gary Hart, Larry O'Brien, had worked on a twenty-four-hour shift to sort it out. And late one night, when Henry had estimated there was approximately two million dollars in unopened letters on the floor of our rattletrap headquarters building, he had hired a couple of guards and had secretly taken the mail to his town house to lock it up in a concrete, fireproof room.

Ironically, on the day after Henry, Mary, and I reminisced about our campaign — which I think was the most honest political campaign in American history — as we sat looking out at the sea, we heard the news that Vice President Spiro Agnew had resigned.

Chapter XII

Living Evidence

In the final days the family crowded together in the forward cabin of the "Dakota Queen II" with George. As in perilous times before, we needed solidarity. It was good to be a unit again.

All of the girls had been campaigning — I doubt if I have ever been prouder than the day Ann, Sue, and Teresa were on the "Today" show. Steve had not joined us on the hustings until then, and I think there were good reasons why. He did not want George to run and did not want him to win — "just give Nixon a scare." He says that the idea of his dad being President "really put me in a cage. I lacked the self-confidence to campaign. And when I read in an article that he had said, 'Steve may be a casualty of the campaign,' I was hurt because it sounded like he was ready to sacrifice his son for the American people."

Ann had been off campaigning alone — necessary
because Wilbur was still in school — leaving her baby
boys at home with the Meads. (Wilbur traveled with
me in the Rhode Island primary, the only time I campaigned with a member of the family.) Like her Aunt
Ila, who had first headed up McGovern volunteers,
then took charge of senior-citizen activities on a national scale, Ann liked chatting informally with those
she called "the forgotten people," the aged who form
such a powerful voting bloc. Soon she started giving
little talks. After her first, she stepped away from the
microphone and inadvertently applauded herself!

Sue and Jim, with Matthew slung over a shoulder or
curled up in a blanket at their feet, had campaigned
nonstop, researching and writing their own speeches,
tackling the issues in a forty-thousand-mile tour, and
were soon bantering with reporters that Matthew had
held more press conferences in five months than Richard Nixon had held since he had been President —
George started telling that story too.

Teresa, by her own admission more outspoken and
outgoing than her sisters and her brother, had been
torn about the public nature of her role in the election.
Yet, in spite of her reticence, she told me, "I'll do what
I can, not just to get Dad elected, but to let him know I
believe in him." Like Sue and Jim, who prepared a
long check list for us to follow to insure that our Washington house was safe, she had acknowledged that
often her legs shook and she grew chilled when the
thought of political assassination crossed her mind.

Mary Kay had insisted that she was going to stay home and it was obvious that she was resentful because she had lost personal time with us for a few more months. But by the middle of September she was canvassing with young Bob Shriver. It was an instructive experience for a young girl to have doors slammed in her face occasionally, such as the time she was charged with "mudslinging" when she tried to explain that George shared the ideals of John Kennedy, Bob Kennedy, Ted Kennedy, Hubert Humphrey, Ed Muskie, and Sargent Shriver, any one of whom, she had been informed by the woman at the door, was preferable to her dad.

There was strange, compelling momentum to the campaign in the last, near-reckless hours, as I flew back and forth across the country with George. We were on an irrevocable journey. For our twenty-ninth wedding anniversary the traveling press corps had given us a Tiffany silver bowl inscribed with George's cry to the crew of his disabled bomber in World War II: "Resume your stations, we're bringing her home!" That is what we were struggling to do, but the landing was in very serious doubt.

It was a time of mindlessness, when it seemed almost normal to be figuring out how to take care of an untrained puppy on the airplane, a gift from a supporter. It was time of instant judgments, when I never questioned speeding insanely across New York expressways, sirens screaming and wheels squealing, clutching the arm of former Mayor Robert Wagner, as we headed toward a rally of thousands who had waited so long for George that I ended up singing over a hand mike to keep them from growing restless. And it was the time of the Hibbing incident, at which point many of my intense feelings came together — about George's efforts, about the people who supported us and my own contribution, and about the press and the schedulers who had been controlling my life.

In New York on the morning of November 1, George was so hoarse he could scarcely speak, his throat was painfully raw, and it appeared doubtful that he could hold to the brutal schedule. The day was planned to start at 6:55 A.M. with an appearance on the "Today" show, then the Barry Farber talk show, an interview with Louisa Quintera of *El Diario,* a ticker-tape parade through the garment district, an International Ladies' Garment Workers' Union luncheon speech, and wheels up for Hibbing, Minnesota, by 3:45 P.M.

I was not surprised when the decision was made for George to spend the afternoon in bed in New York and for me to go to Hibbing in his place. It was to be an important Democratic rally. Senators Muskie, Humphrey, Mondale, Congressman Blatnik, Governor Wendell Anderson, and others would attend, united behind George, who had been scheduled to speak. I felt I had no choice but to go.

Before I left I rode in an open car with George in the big parade through the garment district. It was an incredible spectacle, and we have talked about it often since then. Thousands and thousands of New Yorkers lined the sidewalks, waving, cheering, throwing kisses and bits of paper. Some called, "Good luck, George," or "Eleanor, over here," or "We're for ya!"; others ran up to the convertible and thrust money into our hands. I was elated. It was a tangible sign of the admiration I felt George deserved. It was also a *hopeful* sign — or at least I thought so.

The only way to get to Hibbing was to fly on a chartered jet so small that Skip, the only Secret Service agent able to fit into the plane, sat in the copilot seat, and Mary and I folded up in the back with our luggage banked around us and our briefcases in our laps. We had a speech to prepare. She started jotting down some thoughts; I started writing down mine. I could hardly wait to describe the reception we had received in New York.

About half an hour after takeoff the pilot advised us that we were heading into a severe storm. It had been snowing steadily in Hibbing and airports for miles around were closing. His advice was to make it to Chicago, where the weather was closing in too. Then we could reassess the situation. The irony of flying blindly in the clouds trying to reach the extraordinary Hibbing event did not escape Mary or me, but we congratulated ourselves for being good sports and thought about Margot, who is terrified in small planes and had been lucky enough to stay behind because there had been no space. Not until we started letting down into the Chicago area did we sense that we were in danger.

Then we saw that there was zero visibility. And in our close confinement we could feel the pilot's apprehension. When at last we broke through, we were between tops of buildings, and the runway lights at Midway were to the left of us, not straight ahead. Like a rocket we cut through the narrow gorge of concrete, and veered sharply over toward the ribbon of lights. Heart-stopping seconds passed. When our wheels touched ground, we were barely on the rim of the airfield. A few months later a plane carrying the wife of convicted Watergate burglar Howard Hunt crashed at the same spot.

It was snowing lightly and there was ice on the tarmac as we taxied up to the waiting room for private-aircraft passengers. Inside it was warm and steamy and a few stranded pilots were watching the evening news on the television set in the corner. There we were — George and I — in the middle of the screen, in the center of the panorama in New York, and Herb Kaplow was observing for millions of viewers across the United States that enthusiasm of such magnitude was always good for a candidate personally, but that it probably meant *nothing* politically. I felt sick — and a few days later I told Herb I thought his editorial viewpoint was unfair.

Inside a private office next to the waiting room I found Mary talking long distance to the schedulers. She was obviously furious, and was saying, "I won't take the responsibility, the Secret Service won't take the responsibility, and the pilot *will not fly the plane!*" We stood there and looked at each other. I knew what she was going to say before she said it. "Eleanor, they think you should go to Hibbing, no matter what the circumstances are. But we're going to a hotel instead."

November 7 was a beautiful, crisp day in Mitchell, South Dakota, and George and I went to the polls to vote and over to the campus at Dakota Wesleyan University, where many old friends and colleagues had gathered to wish us well, and then to an assembly at which a chorus of young people sang hymns and George spoke fondly about his ties with the university. Someone asked me to say a few words and I found myself giving a little lecture: "To those of you who say, 'Oh, I can't do this or that,' I want to tell you I've said that to myself a thousand times this past year. But you can. You can do it. This is the amazing thing I've learned about myself, and I'm glad to have found it out, even at my age. Some days in the primaries when I went from five in the morning to midnight, I thought, 'Who do they think I am — a superwoman?' Well, I found out I could do many things — even speak before large audiences, many times not even knowing what I was going to say. You're in a panic, but you get up, and you can do it. That's what I know. You can do it."

Afterward we walked into a few shops downtown. At Burg's shoe store, where I speculated that I had bought hundreds of pairs of children's shoes, someone came up and said, "I used to count eggs for your mother." Ila was walking beside me, and several friends called, "Hi, Eleanor," and she waved back and said, "I'm Ila," and I laughed and called, "I'm Eleanor." Most of our friends did not know what to say, so I filled in for them and kept repeating, "Well, we'll soon know, we'll soon know." After we dropped by at a party for the press at the Minnehaha Country Club, George and the children and I went back to the Holiday Inn to wait for the election results.

I have often wondered if other political wives and their husbands discuss defeat before crucial elections. I do not think many do. It is part of an unspoken contract for each person in a political family to carry a lightning rod of hope until the outcome of a race has been determined. But that afternoon in the motorcade on the way back to the Holiday Inn, as George and Ila and I sat in silence in the back seat of the limousine engrossed in private thoughts, George murmured, "I wonder what it will be like to drive a car again." Ila and I looked at each other, astonished, but nothing more was said.

Neither George nor I nor the children wanted to face the final moment. We did not want to give up until it was absolutely necessary. Even after we went to the auditorium so that George could concede defeat, there seemed to be much more to say. We were surrounded by many, many people who loved us, good people who were as disbelieving as we were. There was no way to reach out or say something personal to each friend. About all I could muster, as I gripped

Skip's arm to keep from stumbling into the limousine outside the auditorium, was to say in a shaky voice, "Well, Skip, perhaps we should have gone to Hibbing after all."

On the way back to Washington Frank Mankiewicz brought us a telegram that Richard Nixon had sent to George. It was very short: "You and Mrs. McGovern have our very best wishes for a well-deserved rest after what I know must have been a very strenuous and tiring campaign." When Mary Kay saw the wire, she cried so hard that she lost her breath, alarming several members of the staff. George leaned over and lightly rubbed her back and said, "She's taking this kind of hard." Mary Kay recalls candidly that she was crying "because I didn't see how anyone in the family — my dad, my mother, my sisters, and my brother — could possibly go back to the life we'd had before. It seemed like we were being forced to go back to a past that didn't fit any more and could satisfy us no longer." I have since assured her that the past seldom fits, and she would probably hate it if it did.

There were more tears a few weeks afterward, when Sue and Jim bundled up Matthew and went to a party. Sue had simply buried her feelings about the campaign; in fact, she had stopped reading the newspapers completely. She was quite unprepared when a guest accosted her and said, "All Presidential campaigns are *bullshit!*" Sue and Jim gathered up Matthew, walked out, and went home. She wept for hours, she says.

I do not know whether that young man believed
what he said or not. According to polls, confidence in
the Presidency rates far below confidence in trashmen;
so I suspect that he did. Perhaps being involved in a
campaign effort would change his perceptions; perhaps not. But if I had been at that party I would have
told him that I believe that as long as people hold politics in low esteem, they are holding their families, their
communities, their country, and, most particularly,
their own integrity in low esteem, and American life
will mirror their values. At least George and I still
believe that our political system will be only as good as
people want it to be.

"I never fully measured the degree of personal
sadness that would come with losing the 1972 election,"
George told me one night after listening to some un-
commonly depressing television news about the state of
the nation. I got up and found one of my notebooks
and a pen. "I want to write down what you have to say
now," I said, "while you are thinking about what 'might
have been.'"

"I think one aspect that still nags me more than anything else," George reflected, "is that each time an eloquent letter comes to me, or some person stops me on
the street to say how much our effort meant to him
personally, I am reminded that we could have filled the
government with devoted people who wanted nothing
more than to serve the interests of the country. To
have missed that opportunity is not easy to accept.

"I will always believe that while every one of us possesses a certain self-interest, the overwhelming majority of the people who gave their energy and their dollars to our campaign did it out of genuine concern for the country. Nothing so horrifies me as the suggestion that patriotism was given a low place in our campaign and a high place in the Nixon campaign. The truth is just the reverse. It was a breakdown of patriotism and respect for the Constitution and for the moral values on which it rests that led us into the predicament that we are in now. The love for country that we found in people who came to rallies and meetings and work sessions, even when the cause seemed futile, is patriotism in action. I think if thirty million people stood up to that kind of test, there are many more potentially within reach of a campaign based on idealism. I still have faith in the essential goodness of people.

"The year of 1972 might have been a last chance for American democracy had it not been for the exposure of Watergate. If the Nixon mandate had been translated into another four years of approval of the kind of special-interest power politics the administration was playing, I am not sure America would have had another chance. I now think we do.

"Occasionally I will run into some young person who will test me, as one did yesterday, saying, 'I broke my back in the 1972 campaign, but I will never do that again. I'm all through trying to change things.' I don't think that she believed that. She wanted to hear what I would say. So I told her, 'You know, I don't agree with you. In many respects I spent all of my life getting ready for 1972, and in that sense it was awfully hard to be defeated, but I am not going to give up.' 'Good!' she said, and did not argue."

That night, when George and I had finished reminiscing, I carefully gathered up my notebook and put it away in the safe with the Fosdick book and the other sentimental objects I value highly. Perhaps the notes will be useful in helping me to explain George's inner vitality when we campaign for our next Senate race. Or maybe I will need perspective as the years go along and our lives turn in new directions. I have no doubt that will happen, and I welcome it. When I trace the inexorable forward movement of my life — the developing child, the coping mother, the growing wife, I see clearly that the present has always been the best of times. And I realize with equal sureness that relationships within marriage, within family, within community, are rich because of their ever-changing character: they assume luster *because* of adversity or perseverance, not in spite of it. With that in mind, it is almost impossible not to reach out again and again. I have stored up years of evidence that affirms there are no endings to the yearnings which move us, only new beginnings.